IWCS Shared Task on Semantic Parsing 2019

Gothenburg, Sweden
24 May 2019

Editors:

Lasha Abzianidze
Rik van Noord
Hessel Haagsma
Johan Bos

ISBN: 978-1-5108-8766-4

Printed from e-media with permission by:

Curran Associates, Inc.
57 Morehouse Lane
Red Hook, NY 12571

proceedings.com

Some format issues inherent in the e-media version may also appear in this print version.

Printed by Curran Associates, Inc. (2019)

For permission requests, please contact the Association for Computational Linguistics at the address below.

Association for Computational Linguistics
209 N. Eighth Street
Stroudsburg, Pennsylvania 18360

Phone: 1-570-476-8006
Fax: 1-570-476-0860

acl@aclweb.org

Additional copies of this publication are available from:

Curran Associates, Inc.
57 Morehouse Lane
Red Hook, NY 12571 USA
Phone: 845-758-0400
Fax: 845-758-2633
Email: curran@proceedings.com
Web: www.proceedings.com

IWCS 2019

Proceedings of the

IWCS Shared Task on Semantic Parsing

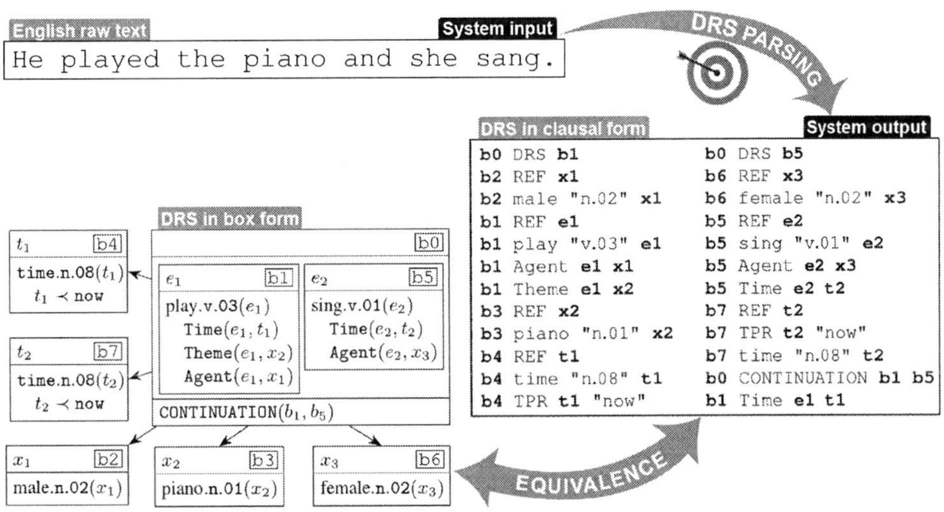

May 24, 2019

Gothenburg, Sweden

Lasha Abzianidze, Rik van Noord, Hessel Haagsma and Johan Bos (eds.)

Proceedings of the IWCS Shared Task on Semantic Parsing

Preface

These workshop proceedings conclude the first shared task on DRS parsing, launched in October, 2018. The workshop was collocated with the 13th International Conference on Computational Semantics (IWCS 2019), held at the University of Gothenburg, Sweden. The goal of the shared task was to produce Discourse Representation Structures (DRSs) for English sentences. Given that DRSs originated from Discourse Representation Theory, a classic theory for studying formal semantics of natural language text, it is difficult to imagine a more suitable topic hosted at IWCS.

DRS parsing is a challenging task, as systems are expected to produce scoped meaning representations involving negation, modals, quantification, and presupposition triggers. Additionally, concepts and event participants in DRSs are described with WordNet synsets and the thematic roles from VerbNet. In this first episode of DRS parsing we tested systems mainly on short, open-domain sentences, to make the threshold for participation as low as possible. We received four system submissions and three system description papers out of 32 registered participants. One system was not described in the workshop paper in order to prevent violating the anonymity clause of the ACL policy for submission. Each system description paper was reviewed by three members of the organising committee – all papers were accepted.

The first shared task on DRS parsing was successful. Despite a small number of submissions, the state-of-the-art results in DRS parsing was moved to a higher level. The variety in methods used (models based on recursive neural networks, transformer models, models based on transition-based parsing, graph decoders) gives inspiration for future series of the shared task.

This is the first time that IWCS hosts a shared task, and we would like to thank the IWCS organizers, the shared task participants and the authors for making this shared task and workshop a successful story!

Shared task page: `https://competitions.codalab.org/competitions/20220`

Workshop page: `https://sites.google.com/view/iwcs2019/shared-task`

Sponsors:

Groningen, 21 May 2019

Lasha Abzianidze
Rik van Noord
Hessel Haagsma
Johan Bos

Table of Contents

DRS parsing

x y
parse.v.01(y)
Result(y, x)
drs.n.01(x)

Workshop Programme
IWCS'19 Shared Task on Semantic Parsing

Location: Asia (1st floor), Wallenberg Centre

14:00	The Parallel Meaning Bank - An Introduction	Johan Bos
14:30	The First Shared Task on Discourse Representation Structure Parsing	Lasha Abzianidze
15:00	Transition-based DRS Parsing Using Stack-LSTMs	Kilian Evang
15:30	Coffee break	
16:00	Discourse Representation Structure Parsing with Recurrent Neural Networks and the Transformer Model	Jiangming Liu
16:30	Neural Boxer at the IWCS Shared Task on DRS Parsing	Rik van Noord
17:00	Reflection and Future Plans	Johan Bos
17:30		
18:00	IWCS opening reception	

The First Shared Task on Discourse Representation Structure Parsing

Lasha Abzianidze Rik van Noord Hessel Haagsma Johan Bos
CLCG, University of Groningen
{l.abzianidze, r.i.k.van.noord, hessel.haagsma, johan.bos}@rug.nl

Abstract

The paper presents the IWCS 2019 shared task on semantic parsing where the goal is to produce Discourse Representation Structures (DRSs) for English sentences. DRSs originate from Discourse Representation Theory and represent scoped meaning representations that capture the semantics of negation, modals, quantification, and presupposition triggers. Additionally, concepts and event-participants in DRSs are described with WordNet synsets and the thematic roles from VerbNet. To measure similarity between two DRSs, they are represented in a clausal form, i.e. as a set of tuples. Participant systems were expected to produce DRSs in this clausal form. Taking into account the rich lexical information, explicit scope marking, a high number of shared variables among clauses, and highly-constrained format of valid DRSs, all these makes the DRS parsing a challenging NLP task. The results of the shared task displayed improvements over the existing state-of-the-art parser.

1 Introduction

Semantic parsing has been gaining in popularity in the last few years. There have been a series of shared tasks in semantic parsing organized, where each task requires to generate meaning representations of specific types: Broad-Coverage Broad-coverage Semantic Dependencies (Oepen et al., 2014, 2015), Abstract Meaning Representation (May, 2016; May and Priyadarshi, 2017), or Universal Conceptual Cognitive Annotation (Hershcovich et al., 2019).

The Discourse Representation Structure (DRS) parsing task extends this development by aiming at producing meaning representations that (i) come with more expressive power than existing ones and (ii) are easily translatable into formal logic, thereby opening the door to applications that require automated forms of inference (Blackburn and Bos, 2005; Dagan et al., 2013). DRSs are meaning representations employed by Discourse Representation Theory (DRT, Kamp and Reyle, 1993). They have been successfully applied for wide-coverage semantic representations (Bos et al., 2004; Bos, 2008), Natural Language Inference (Bos and Markert, 2005; Bjerva et al., 2014), and Natural Language Generation (Basile and Bos, 2013). To the best of our knowledge, there has never been a shared task on scoped meaning representations.

The aim of the task is to compare semantic parsing methods and the performance of systems that take as input an English text and provide as output the scoped meaning representation of that text Since a DRS combines logical (negation, quantification and modals), pragmatic (presuppositions) and lexical (word senses and thematic roles) components of semantics in a single meaning representation, the DRS parsing task shares parts of the following NLP tasks: semantic role labeling, reference resolution, scope detection, named entity tagging, word sense disambiguation, predicate-argument structure prediction, and presupposition projection.

There are only a few previous approaches to DRS parsing. Traditionally, due to the complexity of the task, it has been the domain of symbolic and statistical approaches (Bos, 2008; Le and Zuidema, 2012; Bos, 2015). Recently, however, neural sequence-to-sequence systems achieved impressive performance on the task (Liu et al., 2018; Van Noord et al., 2018), without relying on any external linguistic resources.

SYSTEM INPUT:

Tom isn't afraid of anything.

SYSTEM OUTPUT:

```
b1 REF x1
b1 male "n.02" x1
b1 Name x1 "tom"
b2 REF t1
b2 EQU t1 "now"
b2 time "n.08" t1
b2 NOT b3
b3 REF s1
b3 Time s1 t1
b3 Experiencer s1 x1
b3 afraid "a.01" s1
b3 Stimulus s1 x2
b3 REF x2
b3 entity "n.01" x2
```

BOX FORMAT:

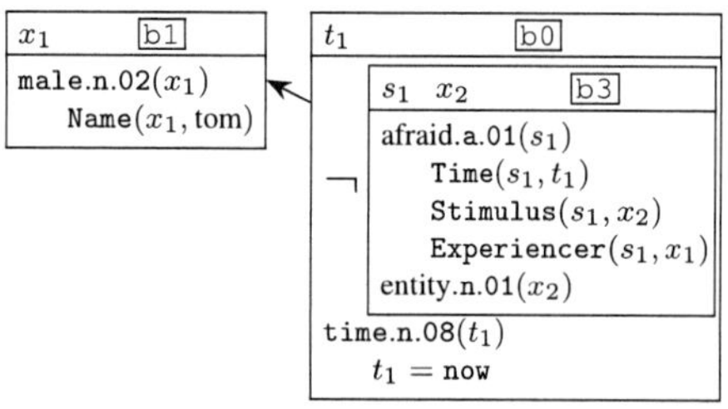

Figure 1: The DRS parsing task: the system input is a short text (the PMB document 99/2308), and the expected output is a DRS in clausal form. Its standard visualisation in box-notation, following DRT, is presented below.

00/3008: He played the piano and she sang.

```
b6 DRS b1                b6 DRS b4
b2 REF x1                b5 REF x3
b2 male "n.02" x1        b5 female "n.02" x3
b1 REF e1                b4 REF e2
b1 play "v.03" e1        b4 sing "v.01" e2
b1 Agent e1 x1           b4 Agent e2 x3
b1 Theme e1 x2           b4 Time e2 t2
b3 REF x2                b4 REF t2
b3 piano "n.01" x2       b4 TPR t2 "now"
b1 REF t1                b4 time "n.08" t2
b1 time "n.08" t1        b6 CONTINUATION b1 b4
b1 TPR t1 "now"          b1 Time e1 t1
```

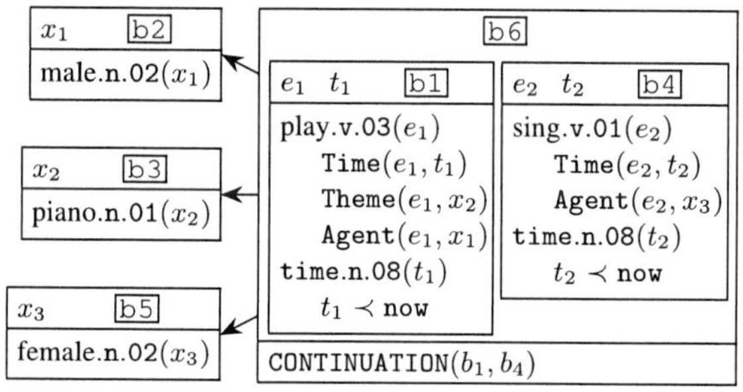

Figure 2: The segmented box b6 consists of a set of labelled boxes, i.e. the discourse segments b1 and b2, and a single discourse condition. In the condition, discourse relation holds between two discourse segments and is formatted in uppercase. The definite noun phrase and the pronouns are presupposition (b2, b3, and b5) triggers.

In the first shared task on DRS parsing, taking into account the information-rich and complex structure of the target meaning representation, we tested participant systems mainly on short, open-domain English texts. In this way, we lowered the threshold for participation to encourage higher results in the shared task and mitigate challenges associated to semantic parsing long texts. In total five systems participated in the shared task. The top-ranked systems outperformed the existing state-of-the-art system in DRS parsing. The shared task was hosted on CodaLab.[1].

2 Task Description

The DRS parsing in a nutshell is presented in Figure 1. Here, the input, a short English sentence, needs to be mapped to the output, a scoped meaning representation in clausal form. Concepts, states and events are represented by the word senses (male.n.02, entity.n.01, afraid.a.01) from WordNet 3.0 (Fellbaum, 1998) and relations are modeled with thematic roles (`Name`, `Experiencer`, `Stimulus`) drawn from an extended version of VerbNet (Bonial et al., 2011).

Each entity needs to introduce a discourse referent, i.e. a variable, in the right scope, form an instance of the right concepts, and be connected to other entities via thematic roles or comparison operators. For example, in Figure 1, *anything* introduces a discourse referent x_2 in the scope b3 with the help of the clause ⟨b3 REF x2⟩. The clause ⟨b3 entity "n.01" x2⟩ makes x_2 an instance of

[1]https://competitions.codalab.org/competitions/20220

entity.`n.01`. Finally, the clause ⟨`b3 Stimulus s1 x2`⟩ connects x_2 to the event entity s_1 of *afraid* via the `Stimulus` thematic role.

The scopes of negation, implication, modal operators or propositional arguments need to be correctly identified. Proper names, pronouns, definite descriptions and possessives are treated as presuppositions and get their own box if they cannot be resolved by the local context. Tense is locally accommodated. For example, Figure 1 shows how the negation operator introduces the scope (`b3`) and how the named entity *Tom* gives rise to the presupposition (`b1`). Figure 2 demonstrates how discourse segments get their own scope (`b1` and `b4`) and how definite noun phrases and pronouns trigger presuppositions (`b2`, `b3`, and `b5`). Finally, Figure 3 depicts an implication with two scopes (`b3` and `b5`), modeling semantics of a universal quantifier, and nested presuppositions (`b1` and `b4`) due to a possessive pronoun.

Given the aforementioned nuances of the fine-grained scoped meaning representations, the DRS parsing task represents a challenge for machine learning methods.

3 Discourse Representation Structure

The meaning representations used in this shared task are based on the DRSs put forward in DRT (Kamp and Reyle, 1993) and derived from the Parallel Meaning Bank (Abzianidze et al., 2017). There are some important extensions to the theory, though. First, the DRSs are language-neutral, and all non-logical symbols are disambiguated to WordNet synsets or VerbNet roles. Furthermore, presuppositions are explicitly represented following (Van der Sandt, 1992) and Porjective DRT (Venhuizen et al., 2018). Discourse structure is analysed following by Segmented DRT (Asher and Lascarides, 2003). As in the original DRT, DRSs are displayed in box format for reading convenience (presuppositional DRSs are displayed with outgoing arrows of the boxes that triggered them). DRSs are recursive structures, and for the purpose of evaluation, they are translated into clauses, flattening down the recursion by reification.

A DRS always contains a main labelled box along with an optional set of presupposition DRSs (see Definition 1). For example, the main labelled box in Figure 1 is `b0` while `b0` is a presupposition. A box can be simple (e.g., the box labelled with `b0` in Figure 1) or segmented (e.g., the box labelled with `b6` in Figure 2). A simple box consists of a set of discourse referents and a set of conditions. Conditions can be basic or complex. Basic conditions are concept predicates or relations over discourse referents and constants. Indexicals are treated as constants, not as discourse referents Bos (2017), for example, *now* is one of such indexicals (see Figure 1). Complex conditions are those involving labelled boxes. The examples of complex conditions are ¬`b3` in Figure 1 and `b3` ⇒ `b5` in Figure 3. Finally, a segmented box contains a set of labelled boxes (`b1` and 4 in Figure 2) and discourse conditions. A discourse condition is a discourse relations over box labels, e.g., `CONTINUATION`(b_1, b_4) in Figure 2.

Definition 1: A BNF of DRSs: (possibly empty) sets are denoted with curly brackets as {⟨ element⟩}. The string elements for operators and punctuation are in red.

⟨*DRS*⟩	::=	{⟨*DRS*⟩} ⟨*labelled BOX*⟩
⟨*labelled BOX*⟩	::=	⟨*label*⟩ ⟨*BOX*⟩
⟨*BOX*⟩	::=	⟨*simple BOX*⟩ | ⟨*segmented BOX*⟩
⟨*simple BOX*⟩	::=	{⟨*discourse referent*⟩} {⟨*condition*⟩}
⟨*condition*⟩	::=	⟨*basic condition*⟩ | ⟨*complex condition*⟩
⟨*term*⟩	::=	⟨*discourse referent*⟩ | ⟨*constant*⟩
⟨*basic condition*⟩	::=	⟨*semantic role*⟩ (⟨*term*⟩, ⟨*term*⟩)
	|	⟨*term*⟩ ⟨*comparison operator*⟩ ⟨*term*⟩
	|	⟨*concept*⟩.⟨*pos_sense_number*⟩(⟨*term*⟩)
⟨*complex condition*⟩	::=	¬⟨*labelled BOX*⟩ | ◇⟨*labelled BOX*⟩ | □⟨*labelled BOX*⟩
	|	⟨*labelled BOX*⟩⇒⟨*labelled BOX*⟩
	|	⟨*discourse referent*⟩:⟨*labelled BOX*⟩
⟨*segmented BOX*⟩	::=	{⟨*labelled BOX*⟩} {⟨*discourse condition*⟩}
⟨*discourse condition*⟩	::=	⟨*discourse relation*⟩ (⟨*label*⟩, ⟨*label*⟩)

01/2312: He put all his money in the box.

```
b1 REF x1                % He [0...2] his [11...14]      b2 IMP b3 b5                % all [7...10]
b1 male "n.02" x1        % He [0...2] his [11...14]      b3 REF x2                   % all [7...10]
b2 REF t1                % put [3...6]                   b3 PartOf x2 x3             % all [7...10]
b2 TPR t1 "now"          % put [3...6]                   b3 entity "n.01" x2         % all [7...10]
b2 time "n.08" t1        % put [3...6]                   b4 REF x3                   % his [11...14]
b5 REF e1                % put [3...6]                   b4 Owner x3 x1              % his [11...14]
b5 Agent e1 x1           % put [3...6]                   b4 money "n.01" x3          % money [15...20]
b5 Theme e1 x2           % put [3...6]                   b5 Destination e1 x4        % in [21...23]
b5 Time e1 t1            % put [3...6]                   b6 REF x4                   % the [24...27]
b5 put "v.01" e1         % put [3...6]                   b6 box "n.01" x4            % box [28...31]
```

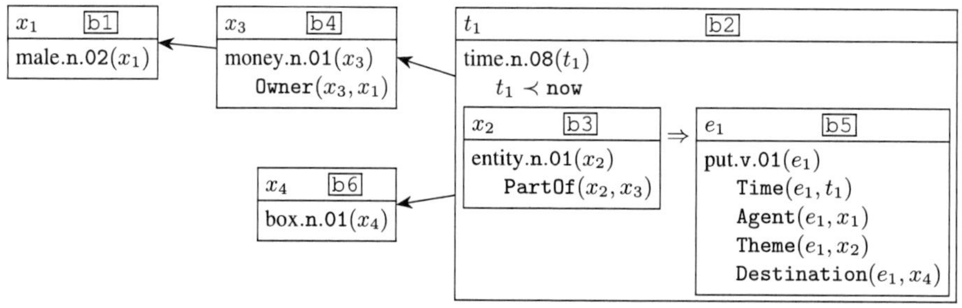

Figure 3: The DRS contains the example of nested presuppositions triggered by the possessive pronoun *his*. The main box b2 of the DRS presupposes a set of two DRSs. At the same time, one of the presupposed DRSs, namely $\langle\{$b1$\},$ b4$\rangle$, itself carries the presupposition b1. Note that the presuppositions about a male discourse referent, triggered by *he* and *his* separately, are merged into a single presupposition box b1. The clauses are accompanied with aligned tokens.

The clausal form and the box-notation are two different forms of displaying scoped meaning representations van Noord, Abzianidze, Haagsma, and Bos (2018). We consider the clausal form a machine-readable format that is suitable for the evaluation with a continuous score between 0 and 1 (see Section 5). On the other hand, the box-notation is a human-readable format and originates from Discourse Representation Theory. Conversion from the box-notation to the clausal form and vice versa is transparent: each box gets a label, and discourse referents and conditions in the clausal form are preceded by the label of the box they occur in.

4 Data

4.1 Released Data

For the shared task we released the training, development, and test data, taken from the Parallel Meaning Bank (PMB, Abzianidze et al. 2017). The PMB is a parallel corpus annotated with formal meaning representations.[2] These representations capture the most probable interpretation of a sentence; no ambiguities or under-specification techniques are employed. The formal meaning representations are automatically constructed and manually corrected. Completely correct representations are flagged as *gold*. Representations that are partly manually corrected are marked as *silver*, while the rest is marked *bronze*.

The PMB release number used for the shared task is 2.2.0[3], of which some statistics are shown in Table 1. Note that MWE tokens and types are underrepresented in the silver and bronze data compared to the gold data. This is because the gold data contains more manual corrections on the token level than the silver and bronze data. For the example of multi-word expressions see Figure 4. In the shared task, participants were allowed to use the silver and bronze data, this would especially make sense in the case of data-hungry neural models, though there is no guarantee that those representations resemble the gold

[2]A part of the corpus can be viewed online via the PMB explorer: `http://pmb.let.rug.nl/explorer`

[3]`https://pmb.let.rug.nl/data.php`

Table 1: Statistics for the PMB release 2.2.0 and the shared task evaluation set.

Data splits	Docs	Tokens	Word types	MWE tokens	MWE types
PMB 2.2.0 gold train	4,597	29,195	4,431	789	494
PMB 2.2.0 gold dev	682	4,067	1,251	71	61
PMB 2.2.0 gold test	650	4,072	1,240	108	100
PMB 2.2.0 silver	67,965	583,835	19,432	4,495	1,902
PMB 2.2.0 bronze	120,662	919,247	23,354	2,054	699
Evaluation set	600	4,066	1,237	92	79

standard.

The data provided to the shared task participants consists of pairs of a raw natural language text and its corresponding scoped meaning representation in clausal form.[4] Whether the meaning representation is of gold, silver or bronze standard is explicitly indicated. To facilitate automatic learning of scoped meaning representations, we also provided automatically induced alignments between clauses and tokens, where token positions are provided with character offsets. The examples of clause-token alignments are give in Figure 2 and Figure 4. The latter represents an exact formatting of the text and clausal form pair provided in the shared task.

```
Nick Leeson was arrested for collapse of Barings Bank PLC.

b1 REF x1                              % Nick~Leeson [0...11]
b1 Name x1 "nick~leeson"               % Nick~Leeson [0...11]
b1 male "n.02" x1                      % Nick~Leeson [0...11]
b2 REF t1                              % was [12...15]
b2 TPR t1 "now"                        % was [12...15]
b2 Time e1 t1                          % was [12...15]
b2 time "n.08" t1                      % was [12...15]
b2 REF e1                              % arrested [16...24]
b2 Patient e1 x1                       % arrested [16...24]
b2 arrest "v.01" e1                    % arrested [16...24]
b2 Theme e1 x2                         % for [25...28]
b2 REF x2                              % collapse [29...37]
b2 collapse "n.04" x2                  % collapse [29...37]
b2 Patient x2 x3                       % of [38...40]
b3 REF x3                              %
b3 Name x3 "barings~bank~plc"          % Barings~Bank~PLC [41...57]
b3 company "n.01" x3                   % Barings~Bank~PLC [41...57]
                                       % . [57...58]
```

Figure 4: A sample of a training document (57/0762). For each document there is a pair of raw text and the corresponding clausal form. Clausal forms incorporate automatically induced clause-token alignment.

4.2 Evaluation set

The official evaluation set contains 600 instances that were not released previously. They will not be released publicly, but are still available for (blind) scoring via the shared task website.[5] However, during the evaluation phase, we asked the participants to provide DRSs for a set of 12,606 short texts. In addition to the raw texts (600) from the evaluation split, this set contained the train (4,597), development (682),

[4]https://github.com/RikVN/DRS_parsing/tree/master/data/pmb-2.2.0
[5]https://competitions.codalab.org/competitions/20220

and test (650) data from the PMB-2.2.0 release and the sentences (6,077) from the SICK dataset (Marelli et al., 2014). The reason for providing the inflated set of raw texts was three-fold: (i) Disguise the raw texts of the evaluation set to make it hard to tune models on them; (ii) Obtain the complete information about the performance of the systems on the provided training, development and test sets; (iii) Carry out extrinsic evaluation of the participant systems on the natural language inference task.

5 Evaluation Metrics and Baselines

Before comparing a system produced clausal form to the gold one, the produced form is checked on validity—whether it represents a DRS. If the clausal form is invalid, it is replaced by a single non-matching clause. In the shared task, we include three baseline systems. The evaluation and validation scripts and the baselines are publicly available.[6]

5.1 Validation

Not all sets of clauses correspond to a well-formed DRS, e.g., discourse referents found in the conditions should be explicitly introduced in the boxes, or there should exist labelled boxes for the labels used in the discourse conditions. We employ the validator REFEREE (Van Noord et al., 2018) to automatically check a set of clauses on well-formedness. REFEREE does several checks for validity checking. For example, first it scans each clause separately in a clausal form and identifies the types of variables based on the operators. For each discourse referent variable, it checks the existence of the binding discourse referent. During this procedure, REFEREE also detects positions of the boxes in the DRS (i.e., so-called the subordinate relation). Based on this information, it is checked that nested boxes do not create loops and there is a unique main box in the DRS.

All the released clausal forms of the DRSs are valid. We provided the participants with REFEREE in order to help them identify the ill-formed clausal forms produced by their systems.

5.2 Evaluation

The evaluation defines to what degree a system output clausal form is similar to the corresponding gold one. To compare the system output and gold representations, we compute the F1-score over the clauses, following Allen et al. (2008). We use the tool COUNTER (van Noord, Abzianidze, Haagsma, and Bos, 2018), which is specifically designed to evaluate DRSs. It is based on the SMATCH Cai and Knight (2013) tool that is used to evaluate AMR parsers. It is essentially a hill-climbing algorithm that finds the best variable mapping between the produced DRS and the gold standard. To avoid local optima, we restart the procedure 10 times. In order to prevent an inflated F-score, before searching the maximal matching, COUNTER discards those REF-clauses which are deemed redundant. A REF-clause $\langle \texttt{b REF x} \rangle$ is redundant if and only if its discourse referent x occurs with a concept predicate in a basic condition of the same box b – in other words, there exists a clause of the form $\langle \texttt{b}\ \ \textit{concept}\ \ \texttt{"}\textit{pos.nn}\texttt{"}\ \ \texttt{x} \rangle$.[7]

An example of comparing the clausal forms of two scoped meaning representations is shown in Figure 5. With respect to the optimal mapping, both, the sample system output and gold clauses, include three clauses that could not be matched with each other while four clauses are matched. The optimal mapping gives us a precision and recall of 3/7, resulting in an F-score of 42.9. Similarly to AMR, we use micro-averaged F-score when evaluating a set of DRSs.

An aspect that is different from the AMR evaluation system is that we generalize over synonyms. In a preprocessing step of the evaluation, all word senses are converted to its WordNet 3.0 synset ID. For example, fox.n.02 and dodger.n.01 both get normalized to dodger.n.01 and are thus able to match.

[6] http://github.com/RikVN/DRS_parsing

[7] In Figure 5 redundant REF-clauses are stricken through.

Sample system output	Optimal mapping	Gold representation
b3 IMP b2 b1	b3 $\mapsto$ b0	b0 IMP b1 b2
~~b2 REF x1~~	b2 $\mapsto$ b1	~~b1 REF x1~~
b2 every "n.01" x1	b1 $\mapsto$ b2	b1 entity "n.01" x1
~~b1 REF x2~~	b0 $\mapsto$ b3	~~b2 REF s1~~
b1 Agent x2 x1	x1 $\mapsto$ x1	b2 Theme s1 x1
b1 new "a.01" x2	x2 $\mapsto$ s1	b2 new "a.01" s1
b1 Time x2 x3	x3 $\mapsto$ t1	b2 Time s1 t1
~~b0 REF x3~~	x0 $\mapsto$ N/A	~~b3 REF t1~~
b0 time "n.08" x3		b0 time "n.08" t1
b3 REF x0		b0 EQU t1 "now"

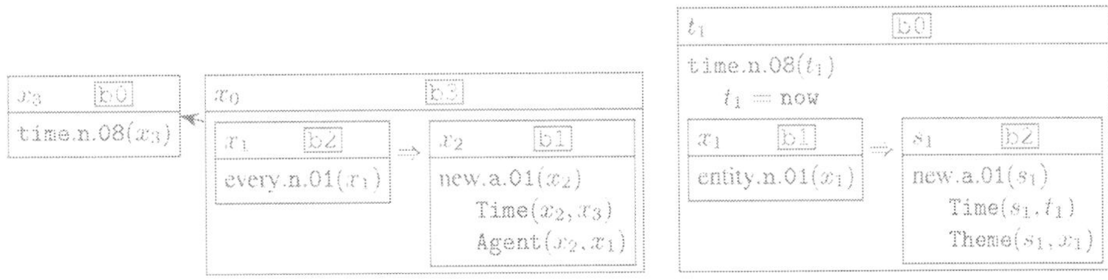

Figure 5: An optimal mapping of variables which maximizes overlap between the system output and gold clausal forms for the sentence (PMB document 00/2302) *Everything is new*. The maximal overlap yields an F-score of 42.9. Matching, non-matching and redundant clauses are in green, red, and stricken through, respectively. The box-notation of scoped meaning representations is not available during the comparison of clausal forms.

To calculate whether two systems differ significantly, we perform approximate randomization Noreen (1989), with $\alpha = 0.05$, $R = 1000$ and $F(model_1) > F(model_2)$ as test statistic for each individual DRS pair.

5.3 Baselines

We provide three baseline parsers: SPAR, SIM-SPAR and AMR2DRS. SPAR simply outputs a default DRS, which is a DRS that is the most similar to the DRSs in our training set.[8] SIM-SPAR outputs the DRS of the most similar sentence in the training set, based on the cosine distance of the average word-embedding vector, calculated using GloVe (Pennington et al., 2014). AMR2DRS is a script that converts the output of an AMR parser to a valid DRS by applying a set of rules, described in Bos (2016) and van Noord, Abzianidze, Haagsma, and Bos (2018). We will provide scores on the development, test and evaluation sets by using the AMR parser of van Noord and Bos (2017).

6 Participating Systems

We received a total of five submissions in the shared task out of 32 registered participants. Three out of five submitted a system paper. The general characteristics of the participating systems are give in Table 2. Following Nissim et al. (2017), we explicitly encouraged the participants to include ablation experiments and negative results (if any). Note that the authors of the systems NOORD ET AL.18 and NOORD ET AL.19 are from the organizers. Below, we provide a short description of each system.

6.1 Van Noord et al. (2018)

NOORD ET AL.18, the parser described in Van Noord et al. (2018), uses a character-level neural sequence-to-sequence model to produce DRSs. They apply a number of methods to improve performance, such as

[8] For PMB release 2.2.0 this is the DRS for *Tom voted for himself.*

Table 2: Overview of the participating systems

	Model	Input	Embeddings	Silver	Bronze
LIU ET AL.	Transformer	char	✗	✓	✓
NOORD ET AL.19	seq2seq	char	✗	✓	✗
NOORD ET AL.18	seq2seq	char	✗	✓	✗
EVANG	stack-LSTMs	word	✓	✗	✗
FANCELLU ET AL.	bi-LSTM	word	✓	✗	✗

rewriting the variables to a more general format, introducing a feature for uppercase letters and *not* using character-level representation for DRS roles and operators. Moreover, they show that performance can be substantially improved by first pre-training on gold and silver data, after which the parser is fine-tuned on only the gold standard data.

6.2 Van Noord (2019)

The system of NOORD ET AL.19 is the parser described in Van Noord et al. (2019) and Van Noord (2019), which follows up on their work previously described in Van Noord et al. (2018). They improve on this work in two ways: (i) by switching their sequence-to-sequence framework from OpenNMT (Klein et al., 2017) to Marian (Junczys-Dowmunt et al., 2018) and (ii) by providing the encoder with linguistic information (lemmas, semantic tags (Abzianidze and Bos, 2017), POS-tags, dependency parses and CCG supertags) that are encoded in a separate encoder.

6.3 Liu et al. (2019)

LIU ET AL. also follow the approach of Van Noord et al. (2018) in terms of pre- and postprocessing the data, but they improve on it by using the Transformer model (Vaswani et al., 2017), instead of a sequence-to-sequence RNN. Also, they show that employing the bronze standard in addition to the gold and silver standard leads to improved performance.

6.4 Evang (2019)

EVANG aim to find a middle-ground between traditional symbolic approaches and the recent neural (sequence-to-sequence) models. They employ a transition-based parser that relies on explicit word-meaning pairs that are found in the training set. Parsing decisions are made based on vector representations of parser states, which are encoded using stack-LSTMs.

6.5 FANCELLU ET AL.[9]

FANCELLU ET AL. propose a graph decoder that given an input sentence encoded via a bidirectional LSTM generates a DAG (Directed Acyclic Graph) as a sequence of fragments from a graph grammar. These fragments are *delexicalized*; predicate names, synset and information on whether the predicate is presupposed or not are predicted in a second step, conditioned on the fragment and the decoding history. Two are the main features of the graph parser: 1) it is agnostic to the underlying semantic formalism and does not need any preprocessing step to deal with variable binding; 2) fragments are aware of the overall graph structure and the graph is built incrementally via a process of non-terminal rewriting. (1) sets this method apart from the graph parser of Groschwitz et al. (2018) where a grammar is extracting via an elaborate pre-processing step, tailored to a specific formalism, whereas (2) allows to leverage neural sequential decoding (stackLSTM, Dyer et al., 2016). The only preprocessing step required is to convert DRSs in clause format into single-rooted, fully instantiated DAGs; we do so by treating both variables

[9]The full list of authors: Federico Fancellu, Sorcha Gilroy, Adam Lopez and Mirella Lapata (University of Edinburgh). Since the authors refrained from submitting a system paper due to the ACL policy for submission, we include a slightly extended summary of their system, generously provided by them.

Table 3: Official results of the shared task for the participating systems

	PMB 2.2.0 (F%)			Evaluation set (%)		
	Train	Dev	Test	Prec.	Rec.	F
AMR2DRS	NA	39.7	40.1	36.7	42.2	38.8
SPAR	NA	40.0	40.8	44.3	35.4	39.4
SIM-SPAR	NA	53.3	57.7	55.7	53.0	54.3
FANCELLU ET AL.	91.1	69.9	73.3	71.9	64.1	67.8
EVANG	84.2	74.4	74.4	71.9	69.9	70.9
NOORD ET AL.18	88.5	81.2	83.3	80.8	78.6	79.7
NOORD ET AL.19	94.9	86.5	86.8	85.5	83.6	84.5
LIU ET AL.	96.9	85.5	87.1	84.8	84.8	84.8

and boxes as nodes and semantic roles, operators and discourse relations as edges between those (where each binary operator or relation gives rise to two edges). Similarly, the only postprocessing step lies in converting the graph back to clause format. This last step can inject errors in the parse and it is the reason why some of the output graphs can be ill-formed.

7 Results

Table 3 shows the official results of the shared task. The system of LIU ET AL. achieved the best performance, though there is no significant difference with the work of NOORD ET AL.19 ($p = 0.23$). The systems of EVANG and FANCELLU ET AL., though clearly outperforming the baselines, are a bit behind the best three systems. However, they can likely improve performance by incorporating silver and bronze standard data. No systems seem to have overfit on the provided dev and test sets. The work of FANCELLU ET AL. is perhaps overfit on the training set, given their high score on train compared to the test sets.

Table 4 shows a more detailed overview of the results. All teams produced a substantial amount of perfect DRSs, but only 31 DRSs of them were perfectly produced by each system. EVANG is the only system with a substantial number of ill-formed DRSs. This hurts their performance, since they get an F-score of 0.0 in evaluation. If we ignore referee and score their ill-formed DRSs as if they were valid, their score increases to 72.1. On the other hand, calculating an F-score for *only* the ill-formed DRSs (without referee) gives us an F-score of 50.6, suggesting that the model would not have scored very well in either way.

Similar as was observed in Van Noord et al. (2018), word sense disambiguation is problematic for the DRS parsers. When assuming oracle sense numbers, all systems obtain a substantially higher F-score (increases of 1.8 to 3.6). NOORD ET AL.19 propose a simple method to improve on this sub-problem by taking the most frequent sense in the training set for a concept, though this only increased their F-scores by 0.2 to 0.4 on the dev and test sets. Nouns are the easiest for all models to correctly produce (possibly due to the frequent `time.n.08`), while adverbs are the hardest, though there are only 12 such clauses in the evaluation set.

8 Analysis

Longer sentences are probably harder to parse, but which systems behave well on longer sentences? Figure 6 shows the performance of the systems plotted over sentence length. As expected, all systems show a clear drop in performance for longer sentences. The work of LIU ET AL. is based on the Transformer model (Vaswani et al., 2017), which claims that performance should not degrade for longer

Table 4: F-scores of fine-grained evaluation of the participating systems on the evaluation set. "Winner out of 5" counts only those instances for which the parser obtained a higher score than all the rest, while "Highest out of 5" allows ties.

	LIU	NOORD19	NOORD18	EVANG	FANCELLU
All clauses	84.8	84.5	79.7	70.9	67.8
DRS Operators	93.9	94.2	91.7	75.2	76.3
VerbNet roles	82.7	83.5	78.1	72.4	66.4
WordNet synsets	83.8	82.3	77.2	67.8	66.5
nouns	89.2	87.5	83.5	75.9	70.3
verbs	69.5	68.9	60.9	44.1	58.3
adjectives	74.8	74.2	66.5	61.5	53.8
adverbs	63.6	45.5	33.3	0.0	31.6
Oracle sense numbers	86.6	87.1	82.6	74.5	69.8
Oracle synsets	90.5	90.7	87.5	80.1	76.5
Oracle roles	88.4	88.5	84.3	74.5	73.7
# of perfect DRSs	214	210	160	95	104
# highest out of 5	383	376	261	171	161
# winner out of 5	100	77	26	18	18
# of ill-formed DRSs	1	0	1	37	5

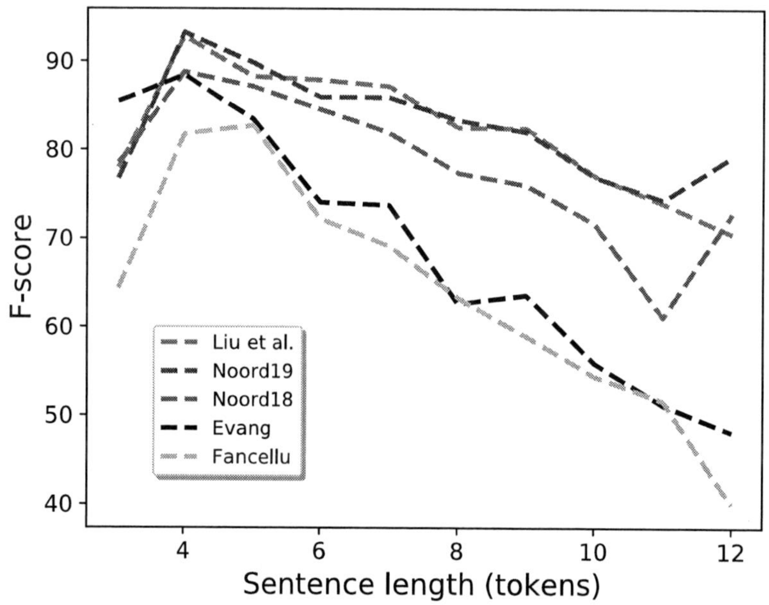

Figure 6: Performance of the systems per sentence length (punctuation are counted as tokens).

sentences. However, for DRS parsing this does not seem to be the case, as LIU ET AL. shows a similar decrease in performance as the neural models of NOORD ET AL.18 and NOORD ET AL.19.

How similar were the outputs of the participating systems to each other? Table 5 shows pairwise comparison of the outputs of the systems on the evaluation set. The only system that has a substantially higher similarity to one of the systems than their official F-score is NOORD ET AL.18 compared to NOORD ET AL.19, which tells us the models make similar mistakes. This makes sense given that they

Table 5: F-scores of all systems compared to each other.

	LIU	NOORD19	NOORD18	EVANG	FANCELLU
LIU		83.4	79.6	70.5	66.6
NOORD19	83.4		83.3	70.9	68.1
NOORD18	79.6	83.3		71.5	67.1
EVANG	70.5	70.9	71.5		61.3
FANCELLU	66.6	68.1	67.1	61.3	

are both character-level sequence-to-sequence models trained on the same data. Additionally, the output of NOORD ET AL.19 comes closest to the output of FANCELLU ET AL. when compared to other systems' outputs. Similarly, EVANG is most similar to NOORD ET AL.18 than to any other systems.

How complementary were the participating systems to each other? If we had an ensemble system, with an oracle component that selected the best DRS for each sentence out of the participants submissions, it would obtain an F-score of 90.5. When only combining the submissions of LIU ET AL. and NOORD ET AL.19, it would already result in an F-score of 89.1. This suggests that the neural models in fact do learn different things, though there is still a significant portion that both methods could not learn.

Finally, are there phenomena that are especially hard for all participating systems? This is not an easy question to answer, and here we show just a first step to such an analysis. Table 6 shows sentences for which systems, on average, performed badly. Some of them show non-standard use of English, others are phenomena that are relatively rare, such as generics, multi-word expressions, and coordination.

Table 6: Sentences for which participating systems, on average, produced the worst DRSs

Sentence	**avg. F**	**Comment**
Thou speakest.	21.4	archaic English
I dinnae ken.	21.8	Scottish
My fault.	24.2	noun phrase
A cat has two ears.	38.1	generic
I look down on liars and cheats.	40.3	coordination, MWE
Get me the number of this young girl.	41.8	imperative
She attends school at night.	44.6	temporal modifier
The union of Scotland and England took place in 1706.	46.4	coordination, MWE
Something I hadn't anticipated happened.	47.0	reduced relative clause
Charles I had his head cut off.	47.2	ordinal, MWE

9 Conclusion

The first shared task on DRS parsing was successful. It improved the state-of-the-art in DRS parsing, and the variety in methods used (models based on recursive neural networks, transformer models, models based on transition-based parsing, graph decoders) gives inspiration for future research. In the future DRS parsing will be made more challenging by moving to longer sentences and texts (where we expect simple seq2seq models to have a harder time), more complex phenomena (ellipsis, comparatives, multi-word expressions), and to languages other than English.

Acknowledgements

We would like to thank the IWCS-2019 organizers, Stergios Chatzikyriakidis, Vera Demberg, Simon Dobnik and Asad Sayeed, for hosting the shared task in Gothenburg. We also would like to thank all participants for their feedback on the task. This work was funded by the NWO-VICI grant "Lost in Translation – Found in Meaning" (288-89-003).

References

Abzianidze, L., J. Bjerva, K. Evang, H. Haagsma, R. van Noord, P. Ludmann, D.-D. Nguyen, and J. Bos (2017, April). The Parallel Meaning Bank: Towards a multilingual corpus of translations annotated with compositional meaning representations. In *Proceedings of the 15th Conference of the European Chapter of the Association for Computational Linguistics: Volume 2, Short Papers*, Valencia, Spain, pp. 242–247. Association for Computational Linguistics.

Abzianidze, L. and J. Bos (2017, September). Towards universal semantic tagging. In *Proceedings of the 12th International Conference on Computational Semantics (IWCS 2017) – Short Papers*, Montpellier, France. Association for Computational Linguistics.

Allen, J. F., M. Swift, and W. de Beaumont (2008). Deep Semantic Analysis of Text. In J. Bos and R. Delmonte (Eds.), *Semantics in Text Processing. STEP 2008 Conference Proceedings*, Volume 1 of *Research in Computational Semantics*, pp. 343–354. College Publications.

Asher, N. and A. Lascarides (2003). *Logics of conversation*. Studies in natural language processing. Cambridge University Press.

Basile, V. and J. Bos (2013). Aligning formal meaning representations with surface strings for wide-coverage text generation. In *Proceedings of the 14th European Workshop on Natural Language Generation*, Sofia, Bulgaria, pp. 1–9.

Bjerva, J., J. Bos, R. Van der Goot, and M. Nissim (2014). The meaning factory: Formal semantics for recognizing textual entailment and determining semantic similarity. In *Proceedings of the 8th International Workshop on Semantic Evaluation (SemEval 2014)*, Dublin, Ireland, pp. 642–646.

Blackburn, P. and J. Bos (2005). *Representation and Inference for Natural Language. A First Course in Computational Semantics*. CSLI.

Bonial, C., W. J. Corvey, M. Palmer, V. Petukhova, and H. Bunt (2011). A hierarchical unification of LIRICS and VerbNet semantic roles. In *Proceedings of the 5th IEEE International Conference on Semantic Computing (ICSC 2011)*, pp. 483–489.

Bos, J. (2008). Wide-Coverage Semantic Analysis with Boxer. In J. Bos and R. Delmonte (Eds.), *Semantics in Text Processing. STEP 2008 Conference Proceedings*, Volume 1 of *Research in Computational Semantics*, pp. 277–286. College Publications.

Bos, J. (2015). Open-domain semantic parsing with Boxer. In B. Megyesi (Ed.), *Proceedings of the 20th Nordic Conference of Computational Linguistics (NODALIDA 2015)*, pp. 301–304.

Bos, J. (2016). Expressive power of Abstract Meaning Representations. *Computational Linguistics 42*(3), 527–535.

Bos, J. (2017, September). Indexicals and compositionality: Inside-out or outside in? In *Proceedings of the 12th International Conference on Computational Semantics (IWCS 2017) – Short Papers*, Montpellier, France. Association for Computational Linguistics.

Bos, J., S. Clark, M. Steedman, J. R. Curran, and J. Hockenmaier (2004). Wide-coverage semantic representations from a CCG parser. In *Proceedings of the 20th International Conference on Computational Linguistics (COLING 2004)*, Geneva, Switzerland, pp. 1240–1246.

Bos, J. and K. Markert (2005). Recognising textual entailment with logical inference. In *Proceedings of Human Language Technology Conference and Conference on Empirical Methods in Natural Language Processing*, pp. 628–635.

Cai, S. and K. Knight (2013, August). Smatch: an evaluation metric for semantic feature structures. In *Proceedings of the 51st Annual Meeting of the Association for Computational Linguistics (Volume 2: Short Papers)*, Sofia, Bulgaria, pp. 748–752. Association for Computational Linguistics.

Dagan, I., D. Roth, M. Sammons, and F. M. Zanzotto (2013). *Recognizing Textual Entailment: Models and Applications*. Synthesis Lectures on Human Language Technologies. Morgan & Claypool Publishers.

Dyer, C., A. Kuncoro, M. Ballesteros, and N. A. Smith (2016). Recurrent neural network grammars. In *Proceedings of the 2016 Conference of the North American Chapter of the Association for Computational Linguistics: Human Language Technologies*, pp. 199–209.

Evang, K. (2019). Transition-based DRS parsing using stack-LSTMs. In *Proceedings of the IWCS 2019 Shared Task on Semantic Parsing*.

Fellbaum, C. (Ed.) (1998). *WordNet. An Electronic Lexical Database*. Cambridge, Ma., USA: The MIT Press.

Groschwitz, J., M. Lindemann, M. Fowlie, M. Johnson, and A. Koller (2018). Amr dependency parsing with a typed semantic algebra. In *Proceedings of the 56th Annual Meeting of the Association for Computational Linguistics (Volume 1: Long Papers)*, pp. 1831–1841.

Hershcovich, D., Z. Aizenbud, L. Choshen, E. Sulem, A. Rappoport, and O. Abend (2019). Semeval 2019 task 1: Cross-lingual semantic parsing with UCCA.

Junczys-Dowmunt, M., R. Grundkiewicz, T. Dwojak, H. Hoang, K. Heafield, T. Neckermann, F. Seide, U. Germann, A. Fikri Aji, N. Bogoychev, A. F. T. Martins, and A. Birch (2018, July). Marian: Fast neural machine translation in C++. In *Proceedings of ACL 2018, System Demonstrations*, Melbourne, Australia, pp. 116–121. Association for Computational Linguistics.

Kamp, H. and U. Reyle (1993). *From Discourse to Logic; An Introduction to Modeltheoretic Semantics of Natural Language, Formal Logic and DRT*. Dordrecht: Kluwer.

Klein, G., Y. Kim, Y. Deng, J. Senellart, and A. Rush (2017). OpenNMT: Open-source toolkit for neural machine translation. In *Proceedings of ACL 2017, System Demonstrations*, Vancouver, Canada, pp. 67–72. Association for Computational Linguistics.

Le, P. and W. Zuidema (2012). Learning compositional semantics for open domain semantic parsing. In *Proceedings of COLING 2012*, Mumbai, India, pp. 1535–1552. The COLING 2012 Organizing Committee.

Liu, J., S. Cohen, and M. Lapata (2019). Discourse representation structure parsing with recurrent neural networks and the transformer model. In *Proceedings of the IWCS 2019 Shared Task on Semantic Parsing*.

Liu, J., S. B. Cohen, and M. Lapata (2018). Discourse representation structure parsing. In *Proceedings of the 56th Annual Meeting of the Association for Computational Linguistics (Volume 1: Long Papers)*, Volume 1, Melbourne, Australia, pp. 429–439.

Marelli, M., S. Menini, M. Baroni, L. Bentivogli, R. Bernardi, and R. Zamparelli (2014). A sick cure for the evaluation of compositional distributional semantic models. In N. Calzolari, K. Choukri, T. Declerck, H. Loftsson, B. Maegaard, J. Mariani, A. Moreno, J. Odijk, and S. Piperidis (Eds.), *Proceedings of the Ninth International Conference on Language Resources and Evaluation (LREC'14)*, Reykjavik, Iceland. European Language Resources Association (ELRA).

May, J. (2016, June). Semeval-2016 task 8: Meaning representation parsing. In *Proceedings of the 10th International Workshop on Semantic Evaluation (SemEval-2016)*, San Diego, California, pp. 1063–1073. Association for Computational Linguistics.

May, J. and J. Priyadarshi (2017, August). Semeval-2017 task 9: Abstract meaning representation parsing and generation. In *Proceedings of the 11th International Workshop on Semantic Evaluation (SemEval-2017)*, Vancouver, Canada, pp. 536–545. Association for Computational Linguistics.

Nissim, M., L. Abzianidze, K. Evang, R. van der Goot, H. Haagsma, B. Plank, and M. Wieling (2017). Sharing is caring: The future of shared tasks. *Computational Linguistics 43*(4), 897–904.

Noreen, E. W. (1989). *Computer-intensive Methods for Testing Hypotheses*. Wiley New York.

Oepen, S., M. Kuhlmann, Y. Miyao, D. Zeman, S. Cinkova, D. Flickinger, J. Hajic, and Z. Uresova (2015, June). SemEval 2015 task 18: Broad-coverage semantic dependency parsing. In *Proceedings of the 9th International Workshop on Semantic Evaluation (SemEval 2015)*, Denver, Colorado, pp. 915–926. Association for Computational Linguistics.

Oepen, S., M. Kuhlmann, Y. Miyao, D. Zeman, D. Flickinger, J. Hajic, A. Ivanova, and Y. Zhang (2014, August). SemEval 2014 task 8: Broad-coverage semantic dependency parsing. In *Proceedings of the 8th International Workshop on Semantic Evaluation (SemEval 2014)*, Dublin, Ireland, pp. 63–72. Association for Computational Linguistics.

Pennington, J., R. Socher, and C. Manning (2014). GloVe: Global vectors for word representation. In *Proceedings of the 2014 conference on empirical methods in natural language processing (EMNLP)*, Doha, Qatar, pp. 1532–1543.

Van der Sandt, R. A. (1992). Presupposition projection as anaphora resolution. *Journal of Semantics 9*(4), 333–377.

Van Noord, R. (2019). Neural Boxer at the IWCS shared task on DRS parsing. In *Proceedings of the IWCS 2019 Shared Task on Semantic Parsing*.

van Noord, R., L. Abzianidze, H. Haagsma, and J. Bos (2018). Evaluating scoped meaning representations. In *Proceedings of the Eleventh International Conference on Language Resources and Evaluation (LREC 2018)*, Miyazaki, Japan.

Van Noord, R., L. Abzianidze, A. Toral, and J. Bos (2018). Exploring neural methods for parsing discourse representation structures. *Transactions of the Association for Computational Linguistics 6*, 619–633.

van Noord, R. and J. Bos (2017). Neural semantic parsing by character-based translation: Experiments with Abstract Meaning Representations. *Computational Linguistics in the Netherlands Journal 7*, 93–108.

Van Noord, R., A. Toral, and J. Bos (2019). Linguistic information in neural semantic parsing with multiple encoders. In *IWCS 2019-13th International Conference on Computational Semantics-Short papers*.

Vaswani, A., N. Shazeer, N. Parmar, J. Uszkoreit, L. Jones, A. N. Gomez, Ł. Kaiser, and I. Polosukhin (2017). Attention is all you need. In *Advances in neural information processing systems*, pp. 5998–6008.

Venhuizen, N. J., J. Bos, P. Hendriks, and H. Brouwer (2018). Discourse semantics with information structure. *Journal of Semantics*.

Transition-based DRS Parsing Using Stack-LSTMs

Kilian Evang
University of Düsseldorf
evang@hhu.de

Abstract

We present our submission to the IWCS 2019 shared task on semantic parsing, a transition-based parser that uses explicit word-meaning pairings, but no explicit representation of syntax. Parsing decisions are made based on vector representations of parser states, encoded via stack-LSTMs (Ballesteros et al., 2017), as well as some heuristic rules. Our system reaches 70.88% f-score in the competition.

1 Introduction

Anyone who complains about arguing over "semantics" has never seen how boring it can be to argue over syntax. —isaacs (@izs). 2013-07-05. Tweet.

A spectrum is haunting semantic parsing—the spectrum ranging from traditional semantic grammars on one end to recent sequence-to-sequence methods on the other. Examples of the former include the LKB system for Minimal Recursion Semantics (Copestake, 2002), and Boxer (Bos, 2008) for Discourse Representation Theory (DRT). Examples of the latter include van Noord and Bos (2017) for Abstract Meaning Representations (AMR) and Liu et al. (2018); van Noord et al. (2018) for DRT. The approach in the present paper aims to occupy a useful middle ground on this spectrum. On the one hand, we emphasize the usefulness of an explicitly specified lexicon of word-meaning pairs, amenable to tweaking by linguists and engineers, and to interfacing with rule-based components. On the other hand, we aim to minimize the amount of grammar engineering required, and rely on neural networks to learn to assemble word meanings into sentence meanings.

We describe a system that follows this approach and apply it to the IWCS 2019 shared task on DRS parsing (Abzianidze et al., 2019). The challenge is to map raw input sentences (plain text, not tokenized or otherwise annotated) to discourse representation structures (DRSs). DRSs represent meaning as a hierarchy of nested boxes containing *referents* and *conditions*. They can be represented as a flat set of *clauses*, where referent identity and special conditions encode the structure. For example, in Figure 1 (top right), all clauses belonging in box **b2** are marked with the **b2** prefix, and that the referent **e1** is introduced by box **b2** is expressed by the special condition **b2** REF **e1**.

Our system is inspired by the AMR parser of Ballesteros and Al-Onaizan (2017) and, by extension, the non-projective dependency parsing algorithm of Nivre (2009): it uses a transition sytem to process tokens from left to right, and stack-LSTMs to create vector representations of parser states to make transition decisions. To apply this approach to DRT, we replace atomic node labels by *lexical clause lists* (LCLs) and edge labels by sets of *referent address pairs* (RAPs), which encode decisions to unify specific discourse referents. We also factor the lexicon to address data sparseness and apply various preprocessing and postprocessing steps to ease learning.

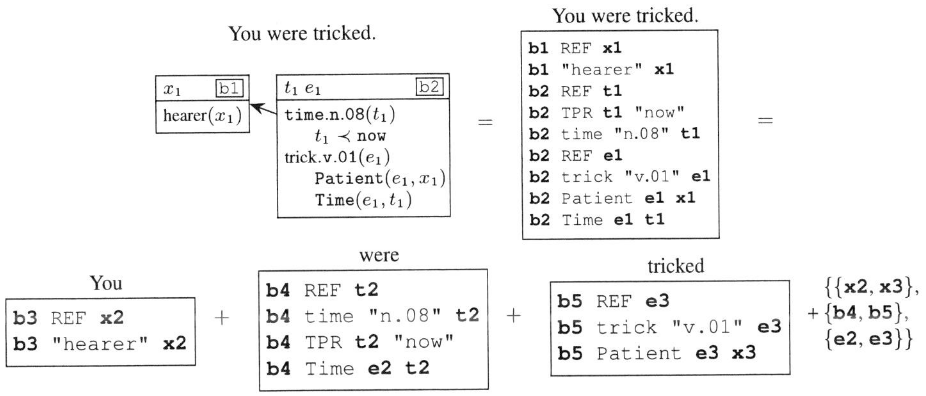

Figure 1: An example DRS in box notation (top left), clause notation (top right), and decomposed into three lexical clause lists (LCLs) and a binding set (bottom row).

Table 1: The most frequent bind actions generated from the shared task gold training data.

rank	action	count	rank	action	count
1	bind({($\mathbf{x}_1$, $\mathbf{x}_1$)})	6 969	6	bind({($\mathbf{b}_1$, $\mathbf{b}_1$),($\mathbf{x}_2$, $\mathbf{x}_1$)})	1 126
2	bind({($\mathbf{b}_1$, $\mathbf{b}_1$)})	3 435	7	bind({($\mathbf{b}_2$, $\mathbf{b}_1$)})	865
3	bind({($\mathbf{x}_2$, $\mathbf{x}_1$)})	2 526	8	bind({($\mathbf{b}_2$, $\mathbf{b}_1$),($\mathbf{s}_1$, $\mathbf{s}_1$)})	644
4	bind({($\mathbf{b}_1$, $\mathbf{b}_1$),($\mathbf{e}_1$, $\mathbf{e}_1$))}	2 187	9	bind({($\mathbf{x}_1$, $\mathbf{x}_2$)})	629
5	bind({($\mathbf{b}_1$, $\mathbf{b}_1$),($\mathbf{x}_1$, $\mathbf{x}_1$))}	1 730	10	bind({($\mathbf{e}_1$, $\mathbf{e}_2$)})	380

2 Parsing Algorithm

Words. They mean things. —The Linguist Llama

For training, we assume tokenized sentences, each paired with a DRS in the form of a clause list, each clause aligned to 0, 1, or more tokens. We decompose this clause list into one *lexical clause list* (LCL) per token, plus a *binding set* $\mathcal{B}$, as shown in the bottom row of Figure 1. Each LCL contains only the clauses aligned to the corresponding token, and referents are replaced by fresh ones unique to that LCL. $\mathcal{B}$ contains all unordered pairs of referents that replaced the same original referent. We say that a referent has an *address* T_n in an LCL if it is the n-th referent of type T to occur in the LCL. For example, **e2** has address $\mathbf{e}_1$ in the LCL for *were*, and **e3** has the same address in the LCL for *tricked*. We write $ref(L, T_n)$ for the referent that has address T_n in L.

The parser uses three data structures: a *stack*, initially empty, a *buffer*, initially containing all tokens of the sentence, and a *result clause list*, initially empty. Until both stack and buffer are empty, the parser repeatedly chooses an *action* that manipulates the contents of the data structures. The correct action sequence for our example is shown in Figure 2. For training, we determine the correct action sequence (also called the *oracle*) as follows: if the rightmost stack element is a token, choose confirm and replace the token with the corresponding LCL. Otherwise, if the rightmost stack element does not contain any referent that still occurs in $\mathcal{B}$, choose reduce, add its clauses to the result clause list, and remove it from the stack. Otherwise, if there are at least two elements on the stack, consider the two rightmost ones; let them be called L and R. Compute the set B of RAPs (referent address pairs) (T_l, T_r) so that $\{ref(L, T_l), ref(R, T_r)\} \in \mathcal{B}$. If B is nonempty, choose bind(B), unify the corresponding referents, and remove referent sets that are now singleton from $\mathcal{B}$. If B is empty and L and R are still in their original order, choose swap and move L to the left end of the buffer. Otherwise, choose shift and move the leftmost buffer element to the rightmost position on the stack.

RAP sets can be seen as an automatically induced approximation to *arguments* in semantic grammars, in that they define the interface between two lexical meaning representations. Table 1 shows the most

action	stack	buffer
init		You were tricked
shift	You	were tricked
confirm	[b1 REF x1 b1 "hearer" x1]	were tricked
shift	[b1 REF x1 b1 "hearer" x1] were	tricked
confirm	[b1 REF x1 b1 "hearer" x1] [b2 REF t1 b2 TPR t1 "now" b2 Time e1 t1 b2 time "n.08" t1]	tricked
swap	[b2 REF t1 b2 TPR t1 "now" b2 Time e1 t1 b2 time "n.08" t1]	[b1 REF x1 b1 "hearer" x1] tricked
shift	[b2 REF t1 b2 TPR t1 "now" b2 Time e1 t1 b2 time "n.08" t1] [b1 REF x1 b1 "hearer" x1]	tricked
shift	[b2 REF t1 b2 TPR t1 "now" b2 Time e1 t1 b2 time "n.08" t1] [b1 REF x1 b1 "hearer" x1] tricked	
confirm	[b2 REF t1 b2 TPR t1 "now" b2 Time e1 t1 b2 time "n.08" t1] [b1 REF x1 b1 "hearer" x1] [b3 REF e2 b3 Patient e2 x2 b3 trick "v.01" e2]	
bind({($\mathbf{x}_1$, $\mathbf{x}_1$)})	[b2 REF t1 b2 TPR t1 "now" b2 Time e1 t1 b2 time "n.08" t1] [b1 REF x1 b1 "hearer" x1] [b3 REF e2 b3 Patient e2 x1 b3 trick "v.01" e2]	
swap	[b2 REF t1 b2 TPR t1 "now" b2 Time e1 t1 b2 time "n.08" t1] [b3 REF e2 b3 Patient e2 x1 b3 trick "v.01" e2]	[b1 REF x1 b1 "hearer" x1]
bind({($\mathbf{b}_1$, $\mathbf{b}_1$), ($\mathbf{e}_1$, $\mathbf{e}_1$)})	[b2 REF t1 b2 TPR t1 "now" b2 Time e1 t1 b2 time "n.08" t1] [b2 REF e1 b2 Patient e1 x1 b2 trick "v.01" e1]	[b1 REF x1 b1 "hearer" x1]
reduce	[b2 REF t1 b2 TPR t1 "now" b2 Time e1 t1 b2 time "n.08" t1]	[b1 REF x1 b1 "hearer" x1]
reduce		[b1 REF x1 b1 "hearer" x1]
shift	[b1 REF x1 b1 "hearer" x1]	
reduce		

Figure 2: Actions for parsing the sentence "You were tricked." Referent addresses (e.g., $\mathbf{b}_1$) should not be confused with referent names (e.g., **b1**).

tricked			
b1 REF **e1** **b1** trick "v.01" **e1** **b1** Patient **e1** **x1** **b1** Time **e1** **t1**	=	**b1** REF **e1** **b1** work "v.00" **e1** **b1** Role **e1** **x1** **b1** Time **e1** **t1**	* [Patient] * trick "v.01"

Figure 3: Factoring a lexical clause list (LCL) into an underspecified lexical clause list (ULCL), a rolelist, and a sense. We use `work "{n,v,a}.00"` as dummy senses.

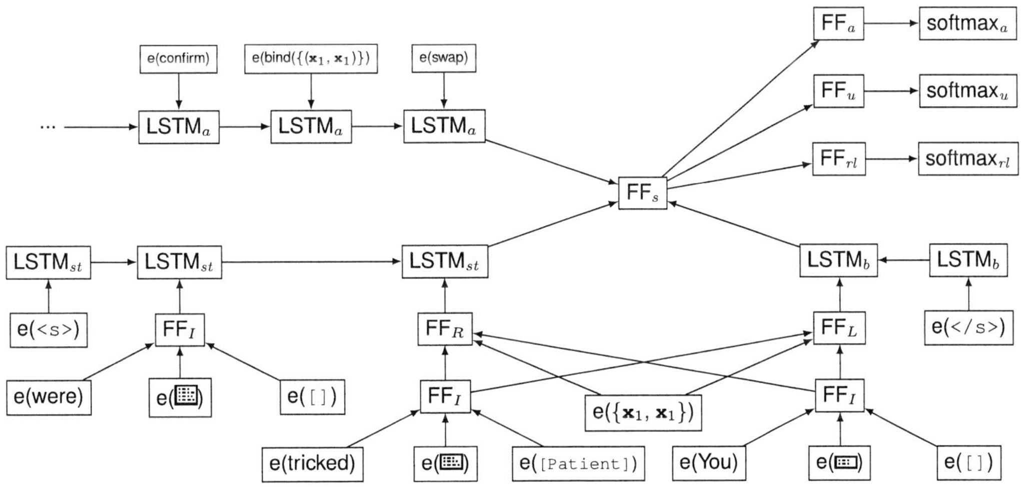

Figure 4: Configuration of the neural network after the second swap action in Figure 2. e(...) are embeddings of words, ULCLs, rolelists, RAP sets, and actions. FF_I is the interpretation function, FF_L, FF_R are the composition functions. Boxes labeled LSTM represent individual LSTM cells of the stack/buffer/action stack-LSTMs. Boxes labeled FF denote feed-forward neural networks with one hidden layer; FF_s has a RelU nonlinearity and the others have a tanh nonlinearity.

frequent bind actions. In total, 127 were induced from the training data. They may be too sparse. Our RAP set generation is not sensitive to referent names since referents are addressed by order, not name. However, it is sensitive to clause order and referent type. As a reviewer pointed out, van Noord et al. (2018) showed that normalizing clause order while conflating the referent types **x**, **t**, and **e** improved performance in their parser. We plan to investigate this in future work.

3 Parsing Model

At test time, we have neither gold-standard LCLs nor a binding set, yet we want to end up with a result clause list that is the same as the gold standard DRS, or at least similar. We thus train a statistical model to choose the right action at each parser state, and to choose the right lexical clause list for each token. The model has three softmax classifiers, shown in the top right corner of Figure 4: the *action classifier*, the *ULCL classifier*, and the *rolelist classifer*. At each state, the action classifier chooses one out of 131 actions which were extracted from the shared task gold training data, 127 of which are bind actions with various RAP sets. The classifier only chooses among the actions which are applicable to the respective state, for example, shift requires a nonempty buffer, and bind actions require every addressed referent to exist. After each confirm action, the model chooses an LCL for the token on the stack to be replaced with.

To better handle the large variety of LCLs, we factor this into three steps, as illustrated in Figure 3: first, the *ULCL classifier* chooses one out of 548 different ULCLs (underspecified LCLs with dummy event roles, dummy senses, and dummy constants). The *rolelist classifier* then chooses from 146 lists of event roles to replace the dummy event roles with. Finally, heuristic rule-based components ("symbolizers", see below) fill in the senses and constants.

The set of ULCLs is automatically created offline from all LCLs in the training data by normalizing referent names and replacing event roles, senses, and constants with dummy values. Non-event roles are currently left intact, as are a number of very common senses and constants (`male "n.02"`, `female "n.02"`, `time "n.08"`, `person "n.01"`, `measure "n.02"`, `entity "n.01"`, `country "n.02"`, `city "n.01"`, `quantity "n.01"`, `name "n.01"`, `location "n.01"`, `"now"`, `"speaker"`, `"hearer"`).

The input to the three classifiers is a vector representation of the parser state, computed using *stack-LSTM* representations of the stack, the buffer, and the list of previous actions. Stack-LSTMs (Ballesteros et al., 2017; Ballesteros and Al-Onaizan, 2017) are LSTMs (Hochreiter and Schmidhuber, 1997) whose sequence of input vectors can change dynamically. Over the course of a parsing process, the parser grows and shrinks these input sequences as elements are added to and removed from the associated data structures. Initially, the buffer LSTM (LSTM_b) has the word embeddings of the entire input sequence. These are gradually moved to the stack LSTM (LSTM_{st}) by shift actions, where they are further transformed: when confirm occurs, the righmost hidden state of the stack LSTM is transformed by an *interpretation function* and its output then replaces the rightmost input to the stack-LSTM. When bind occurs, the two rightmost hidden states of LSTM_{st} are transformed by two separate *composition functions* and their outputs replace the two rightmost inputs to the LSTM_{st}. Inputs to LSTM_{st} can also become inputs to LSTM_b again through swap actions. Figure 4 shows one snapshot of the dynamically changing network, after the second swap action in our example.

4 Implementation

Our system is implemented in Python using DyNet (Neubig et al., 2017). We use ELMo (Peters et al., 2018) for pre-trained word embeddings. At test time, we tokenize sentences using Elephant (Evang et al., 2013) trained on a pre-release version of the Parallel Meaning Bank (Abzianidze et al., 2017).

Hyperparameters Time did not allow for extensive tuning. Where applicable, we followed the choices of Ballesteros et al. (2017). For details, see Table 2 and the source code (`https://bitbucket.org/kevang/drs_parsing`).

Preprocessing and Postprocessing In the training data, the constants `"speaker"` and `"hearer"` typically appear in clauses aligned to verbs rather than first and second person pronouns. To prevent a proliferation of verb ULCLs, our system changes this representation to the one shown in Figure 1 for training and applies an inverse transformation to its output at test time. It also creates a "main box" (a DRS containing all other DRSs) in postprocessing if none exists yet.

Symbolizers We implemented rule-based components that replace dummy constants with proper constants for names (e.g., `"mary"` for the token `Mary`), quantities (e.g., `"1000"` for the token `"one~thousand"`), and time expressions (e.g., `"05:00"` for the token `five~o'clock`). For

Table 2: Hyperparameter settings.

hyperparameter	value
updated word embeddings	
unknown word probability	0.2
dimensions	40
pretrained word embeddings (ELMo)	
dimensions (average of 3 layers)	1024
other embedding dimensions	
actions	20
ULCLs	20
RAP sets	20
rolesets	20
stack-LSTMs	
input dimensions	100
hidden layers	2
hidden dimensions (per layer)	100
learning rate (simple SGD)	
initial value	0.1
decay per epoch	0.08

dummy word senses, we fill in the lemma using NLTK's WordNet lemmatizer (Bird et al., 2009) and assume sense number `01`.

Training We train with 1 batch = 1 training example, using the negative sum of the log probabilities of all correct classification decisions as loss. We train on the gold training data for 20 epochs and validate after each epoch on the gold development data using Counter (van Noord et al., 2018). We use the model with the highest validation f-score.

5 Competition Results and Discussion

For the competition, we used the best model unchanged, i.e., we did not retrain with the dev/test data included. At this point, our system had a bug where the interpretation function FF_I only took ULCL and rolelist embeddings as input, not the word embedding. It was also still lacking the quantity symbolizer. It reached 74.34% precision, 73.32% recall, and 73.83% f-score on the development data, 74.60% precision, 74.14% recall, and 74.37% on the test data, and 71.81%, 69,92% recall, and 70.88% f-score in the competition. The organizers provided five sentences for which our system's output was lowest (highest) compared to the minimum (maximum) of the other participating systems, along with all outputs. We inspected sentences and tried to identify the main reasons our system performed worse (better) than others on these examples. They are by no means guaranteed to be representative, but may serve as starting points for discussion and further investigation.

Reasons for Failure (a) The system "skipped" some tensed matrix verbs, i.e., it assigned them the empty ULCL, as it does for punctuation (sentences 522, 271, 385). This may point to failure to generalize or sparse data. (b) The system introduced many DRSs but failed to connect them by binding referents, so it defaulted to connect them with CONTINUATION discourse relations in post-processing (452, 414).

Reasons for Success (c) The system profited from the decision to leave special senses intact, which enabled it to correctly analyze relational nouns (309). (d) The system was not completely thrown off by archaic language, possibly helped by the large body of text the ELMo embeddings are trained on (163). (e) A rare adjective seemed to trip up character-based systems, but was handled correctly by our WordNet-based symbolizer (147). (f) Our system's first-sense heuristic got lucky (454). (g) Our system got lucky and agreed with an apparent error in the gold standard (138).

We further observe that our system does very poorly on some sentences that lack sentence-final punctuation, which points to hypersensitivity to diversions that is typical of current neural models (cf., e.g., Søgaard et al., 2018). Our current oracle generation algorithm treats anaphora like other long-distance dependencies, which we surmise is suboptimal. Finally, the shared task data has quite an aggressive approach to merging multi-token units into a single token, which is not handled optimally by the tokenizer we used. Beyond these specific avenues for future improvement, generic ones are applicable: architecture optimization, hyperparameter optimization, ensembles, additional features from taggers and dependency parsers, training on silver data, etc. Some of these have been shown to have a large impact on similar tasks (Ballesteros and Al-Onaizan, 2017; van Noord et al., 2018).

6 Ablations

After the competition, we improved the system by fixing the bug in the interpretation function and adding the quantity symbolizer. We then ran an ablation study to assess the contribution of some individual components. The results are shown in Table 3. Contrary to our expectations, factoring rolelists out of ULCLs does not seem to improve results, although it helps the system reach its peak performance after

	precision	recall	f-score	epochs
full system	.7562	.7460	.7511	15
- factoring rolelists out of ULCLs	.7545	.7503	.7524	18
- realigning pronouns	.7545	.7444	.7494	20
- date/time symbolizer	.7535	.7434	.7484	15
- quantity symbolizer	.7495	.7395	.7445	15

Table 3: Ablation results on the development data, with one component removed at a time. "Epochs" indicates the number of training epochs needed to reach the indicated f-score.

fewer epochs. Realigning pronouns helps a bit. The date/time symbolizer and the quantity symbolizer are clearly beneficial.

7 Conclusions

Traditional semantic grammars are transparent, but theory-heavy and costly to adapt to new languages and domains. End-to-end systems are easy to use and performant, but opaque: if there are errors, it is hard to pinpoint the causes and fix them. Thus, either approach has problems that may make it infeasible in production, semi-automatic annotation, or education settings. We believe that our approach—lexicalist but with no need for an explicit representation of syntax—strikes an elegant balance between the two extremes. At the time of this writing, we do not know where our system ranks among the shared task participants. Previous work on similar tasks (Liu et al., 2018; van Noord et al., 2018) has reached f-scores of up to 77.5% resp. 83.6%, however, these results were obtained on different and potentially less complex test sets. And as discussed above, there are many promising avenues to further increasing the performance of our system. Thus, whatever the outcome of this competition, we believe that our approach is worth pursuing further.

Acknowledgments

The author would like to thank the three anonymous reviewers for valuable feedback. This work was carried out within the TreeGraSP project, funded by a Consolidator Grant of the European Research Council.

References

Abzianidze, L., J. Bjerva, K. Evang, H. Haagsma, R. van Noord, P. Ludmann, D.-D. Nguyen, and J. Bos (2017). The Parallel Meaning Bank: Towards a multilingual corpus of translations annotated with compositional meaning representations. In *Proceedings of the 15th Conference of the European Chapter of the Association for Computational Linguistics: Volume 2, Short Papers*, pp. 242–247. Association for Computational Linguistics.

Abzianidze, L., R. van Noord, H. Haagsma, and J. Bos (2019). The first shared task on discourse representation structure parsing. In *Proceedings of the IWCS 2019 Shared Task on Semantic Parsing*.

Ballesteros, M. and Y. Al-Onaizan (2017). AMR parsing using stack-LSTMs. In *Proceedings of the 2017 Conference on Empirical Methods in Natural Language Processing*, pp. 1269–1275. Association for Computational Linguistics.

Ballesteros, M., C. Dyer, Y. Goldberg, and N. A. Smith (2017). Greedy transition-based dependency parsing with stack lstms. *Computational Linguistics, Volume 43, Issue 2 - June 2017*, 311–347.

Bird, S., E. Loper, and E. Klein (2009). *Natural Language Processing with Python.* O'Reilly Media Inc.

Bos, J. (2008). Wide-coverage semantic analysis with Boxer. In *Semantics in Text Processing. STEP 2008 Conference Proceedings.*

Copestake, A. (2002). *Implementing typed feature structure grammars*, Volume 110. Stanford: CSLI.

Evang, K., V. Basile, G. Chrupała, and J. Bos (2013). Elephant: Sequence labeling for word and sentence segmentation. In *Proceedings of the 2013 Conference on Empirical Methods in Natural Language Processing*, pp. 1422–1426. Association for Computational Linguistics.

Hochreiter, S. and J. Schmidhuber (1997, November). Long short-term memory. *Neural Comput. 9*(8), 1735–1780.

Liu, J., S. B. Cohen, and M. Lapata (2018). Discourse representation structure parsing. In *Proceedings of the 56th Annual Meeting of the Association for Computational Linguistics (Volume 1: Long Papers)*, pp. 429–439. Association for Computational Linguistics.

Neubig, G., C. Dyer, Y. Goldberg, A. Matthews, W. Ammar, A. Anastasopoulos, M. Ballesteros, D. Chiang, D. Clothiaux, T. Cohn, K. Duh, M. Faruqui, C. Gan, D. Garrette, Y. Ji, L. Kong, A. Kuncoro, G. Kumar, C. Malaviya, P. Michel, Y. Oda, M. Richardson, N. Saphra, S. Swayamdipta, and P. Yin (2017). DyNet: The dynamic neural network toolkit. *arXiv preprint arXiv:1701.03980.*

Nivre, J. (2009). Non-projective dependency parsing in expected linear time. In *Proceedings of the Joint Conference of the 47th Annual Meeting of the ACL and the 4th International Joint Conference on Natural Language Processing of the AFNLP*, pp. 351–359. Association for Computational Linguistics.

Peters, M. E., M. Neumann, M. Iyyer, M. Gardner, C. Clark, K. Lee, and L. Zettlemoyer (2018). Deep contextualized word representations. In *Proc. of NAACL.*

Søgaard, A., M. de Lhoneux, and I. Augenstein (2018, November). Nightmare at test time: How punctuation prevents parsers from generalizing. In *Proceedings of the 2018 EMNLP Workshop BlackboxNLP: Analyzing and Interpreting Neural Networks for NLP*, Brussels, Belgium, pp. 25–29. Association for Computational Linguistics.

van Noord, R., L. Abzianidze, H. Haagsma, and J. Bos (2018). Evaluating scoped meaning representations. In *Proceedings of the Eleventh International Conference on Language Resources and Evaluation (LREC 2018)*, Miyazaki, Japan.

van Noord, R., L. Abzianidze, A. Toral, and J. Bos (2018). Exploring neural methods for parsing discourse representation structures. *Transactions of the Association for Computational Linguistics 6*, 619–633.

van Noord, R. and J. Bos (2017). Neural semantic parsing by character-based translation: Experiments with abstract meaning representations. *Computational Linguistics in the Netherlands Journal 7*, 93–108.

Discourse Representation Structure Parsing with Recurrent Neural Networks and the Transformer Model

Jiangming Liu Shay B. Cohen Mirella Lapata
Institute for Language, Cognition and Computation
School of Informatics, University of Edinburgh
10 Crichton Street, Edinburgh EH8 9AB
jiangming.liu@ed.ac.uk, {scohen,mlap}@inf.ed.ac.uk

Abstract

We describe the systems we developed for Discourse Representation Structure (DRS) parsing as part of the IWCS-2019 Shared Task of DRS Parsing.[1] Our systems are based on sequence-to-sequence modeling. To implement our model, we use the open-source neural machine translation system implemented in PyTorch, OpenNMT-py. We experimented with a variety of encoder-decoder models based on recurrent neural networks and the Transformer model. We conduct experiments on the standard benchmark of the Parallel Meaning Bank (PMB 2.2.0). Our best system achieves a score of 84.8% F_1 in the DRS parsing shared task.

1 Introduction

Discourse Representation Theory is a popular theory of meaning representation designed to account for a variety of linguistic phenomena, including the interpretation of pronouns and temporal expressions within and across sentences (Kamp and Reyle, 1993). The Groningen Meaning Bank (GMB; Bos et al. 2017) provides a large collection of English texts annotated with Discourse Representation Structures (DRS), while the Parallel Meaning Bank (PMB; Abzianidze et al. 2017) provides DRSs in English, German, Italian and Dutch. Furthermore, the PMB introduces clause representation, as shown on the top of Figure 1.

With the recent introduction of neural network learning to the Natural Language Processing community, several neural DRS parsers have been developed for the problem of DRS parsing, i.e. the problem of taking a document or a sentence as input, and outputting their corresponding DRS. Liu et al. (2018) convert box-style DRSs to tree-style DRSs and propose the three-step tree DRS parser on the GMB, while van Noord et al. (2018) adopt a neural machine translation approach to parse sentences to their clause-style DRSs on PMB. Due to the different standard of annotations between GMB and PMB, and that the IWCS-2019 Shared Task of DRS Parsing mainly focuses on averagely short sentences in PMB annotations, our systems take sentences as input and output a clause-style DRS of PMB represented as a sequence for the IWCS-2018 Shared Task of DRS parsing (Abzianidze et al., 2019).

2 The Parsing System

Figure 2 shows the data pipeline in our system for both training and parsing. There are three main parts: (a) The component **Preprocess**, which prepares the input data to make it suitable for training and parsing models; (b) The component **Neural Model** which is based on OpenNMT; (c) The component **Postprocess** which contains some rules to ensure the system output is a well-formed DRSs.

[1] https://competitions.codalab.org/competitions/20220

```
b1 REF e1                    b1 live "v.01" e1
b1 REF t1                    b1 time "n.08" t1
b1 EQU t1 "now"              b1 Location e1 x1
b1 Theme e1 "speaker"        b2 REF x1
b1 Time e1 t1                b2 ground_floor "n.01" x1
```

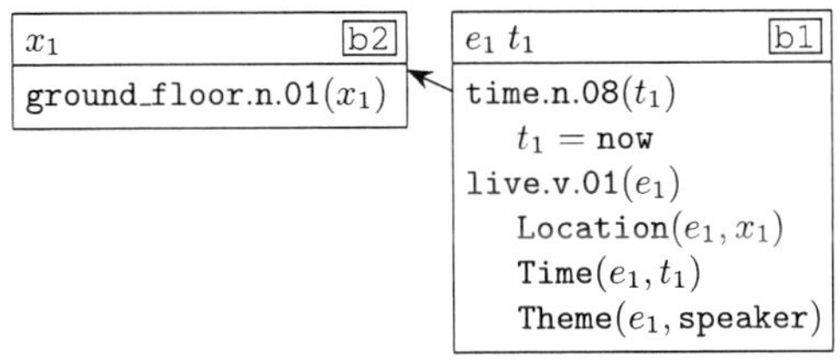

Figure 1: The clause representations (top) and box-style representations (bottom) for the sentence *I live on the ground floor.*.

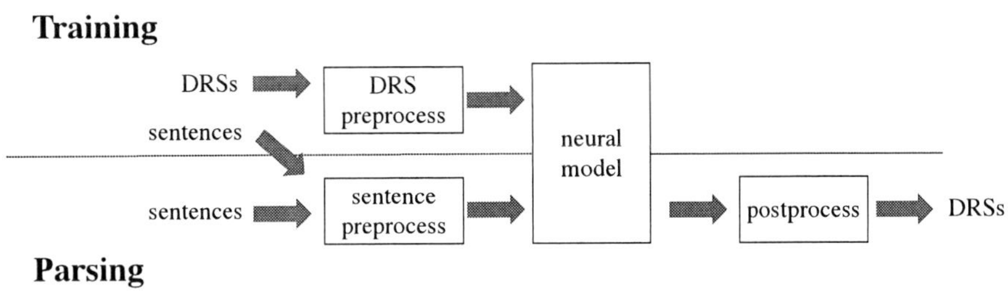

Figure 2: The framework of our DRS parsing system.

2.1 Preprocessing

The **Preprocess** step works on the sentences and their DRSs of the training data and on the sentences of the development and the test data. We tried two levels of preprocessing, character-level and word-level.

Character Level We use the scripts of van Noord et al. (2018) to perform character-level preprocessing for sentences and their DRSs. Each sentence is separated into characters where a special symbol "|||" is used to mark a word boundary.[2] The clauses are represented as a character sequence, except for the semantic roles, DRS operators and deictic constants, as shown in Figure 3(a). For example, "**b1** REF **e1**" is preprocessed to "**$NEW** ||| REF", which means that a new box (**b1**) is construct and a new referent (**e1**) is introduced by the box; "**b2** ground_floor "n.01" **x1**" is preprocessed to "**$0** ||| g r o u n d _ f l o o r ||| " n . 0 1 " ||| **@0**", which means that the sense *ground_floor.n.01* is constructed and then assigned to the referent **@0**, which is latest introduced, where **@n** (n$\in \mathbb{Z}$) denotes the referent $|n|$th latest introduced.[3]. Similarly, **$n** (n$\in \mathbb{Z}$) denotes the box $|n|$th latest constructed.

Word Level Each sentence is tokenized using the Moses script[4] and then transformed to its lowercase form. Clauses are represented as sequences without changing the order, where a special symbol "|||" is used to start a new clause. We rule out quotation marks in clauses (e.g. *"tom"* is converted to *tom*) and

[2]Here, sentences are not further tokenized than they are in the data, and a token could be *I'm* or *floor.* .

[3]if n is positive, **@n** denotes the referent is nth latest introduced in future.

[4]`https://github.com/moses-smt/mosesdecoder`

sentence: i ||| l i v e ||| o n ||| t h e ||| g r o u n d ||| f l o o r .
DRS: **$NEW** ||| REF *** **$0** ||| REF *** **$0** ||| EQU ||| **@0** ||| "now" *** **$0** ||| Theme ||| **@-1** ||| "speaker" *** **$0** ||| Time ||| **@0** ||| **@-1** *** **$0** ||| l i v e ||| " v . 0 1 " ||| **@-1** *** **$0** ||| t i m e ||| " n . 0 8 " ||| **@0** *** **$0** ||| Location ||| **@-1** ||| **@1** *** **$NEW** ||| REF *** **$0** ||| g r o u n d _ f l o o r ||| " n . 0 1 " ||| **@0**

(a) character level

sentence: i live on the ground floor .
DRS: **$NEW** REF ||| **$0** REF ||| **$0** EQU **@0** now ||| **$0** Theme **@-1** speaker ||| **$0** Time **@0** **@-1** ||| **$0** live v.01 **@-1** ||| **$0** time n.08 **@0** ||| **$0** Location **@-1** **@1** ||| **$NEW** REF ||| **$0** ground_floor n.01 **@0**

(b) word level

Figure 3: An example of preprocessing in character level and word level, respectively.

LSTM					
Parameter	Value	Parameter	Value	Parameter	Value
layers	2	batch_size	12	global_attention	general
rnn_size	300	batch_type	sents	copy_attention	True
rnn_type	LSTM	optim	sgd	copy_attn_type	dot
dropout	0.2	learning_rate	0.7	start_decay_steps	5000
bridge	True	learning_rate_decay	0.7	decay_steps	1000
encoder_type	brnn	max_grad_norm	5	decoder_type	rnn
Transformer					
Parameter	Value	Parameter	Value	Parameter	Value
layers	6	batch_size	512	encoder_type	transformer
rnn_size	300	batch_type	tokens	decoder_type	transformer
transformer_ff	2048	optim	adam	position_encoding	True
heads	6	learning_rate	0.001	copy_attn_type	dot
dropout	0.2	global_attention	general	max_grad_norm	5
bridge	True	copy_attention	True		

Table 1: Choice of hyperparameters for our neural network models.

remain them case-sensitive. Following previous work (van Noord et al., 2018), the indices of variables in clauses are relative, as shown in Figure 3(b), which is the same to the character-level preprocessing.

2.2 Neural Models

We adopt Recurrent Neural Networks (RNNs) equipped with Long Shot-Term Memory (LSTM; Hochreiter and Schmidhuber 1997) units and the Transformer model (Vaswani et al., 2017) as our neural models. For the model implementation, we use the one provided by the OpenNMT-py toolkit (Klein et al., 2017). The hyperparameters we used are shown in Table 1 which are institutionally set without optimization.

Fine-tuning We propose a fine-tuning approach to enable the system to effectively use more training data in various quality, i.e. bronze and silver data. The fine-tuning approach allows the system train to convergence on one dataset (e.g. silver and gold data) and then continues to train to convergence on another dataset (e.g. gold data), where the optimizers are reset.

LSTM	character				word			
	P	R	F1	time(h)	P	R	F1	time(h)
sg-data	73.91	75.00	74.45	13.1	73.81	73.75	73.78	7.8
sg-data + g-data	86.05	84.78	85.41	+2.0	84.80	82.83	83.80	+0.8
Transformer	**character**				**word**			
	P	R	F1	time(h)	P	R	F1	time(h)
sg-data	69.11	69.93	69.52	5.2	75.41	75.36	75.38	5.1
sg-data + g-data	82.32	81.19	81.75	+0.6	85.76	84.45	85.10	+0.6

Table 2: Results on test partition of the Parallel Meaning Bank.

	P	R	F1
bsg-data	74.27	75.78	75.02
bsg-data + sg-data	77.74	78.78	78.26
bsg-data + g-data	86.98	86.55	86.76
bsg-data + sg-data + g-data	87.04	87.17	87.10

Table 3: Results on test dataset by word transformer

2.3 Postprocessing and Evaluation

We adopt the postprocessing scripts of van Noord et al. (2018) to transform back the output of our models to the clause format, and then use COUNTER (van Noord et al., 2018) as our evaluation metric.

3 Experiments

In this section, we introduce the training data that we used and the results on the PMB benchmarks.

3.1 Data

The training data consists of all of the bronze data (bronze), all of the silver data (silver), and the training section of the gold data (gold). All data is preprocessed. We mix bronze, silver and gold as **bsg-data**, and mix silver and gold as **sg-data**, and name the training section of gold data as **g-data**. Meanwhile, we adopt GloVe (Pennington et al., 2014) pre-trained word embeddings[5] to initialize the representation of input tokens.

3.2 Results

Table 2 shows the results on test data, where **sg-data** means that the models are only trained on **sg-data**, and **+ g-data** means that the models are continually fine-tuned on **g-data**. With LSTM, the character model performs marginally better than the word model. However, with Transformer, the word model performs significantly better than the character model. With both LSTM and Transformer, fine-tuning on **g-data** significantly improves the performance. Although the character LSTM is marginally better than the word Transformer, we still prefer the word Transformer as our final model, because it could be trained faster.

Table 3 shows the improved results on test dataset by using word Transformer with bronze data, where **bsg-data** means that the model is only trained on **bsg-data**, **+ sg-data** means that the model is continually fine-tuned on **sg-data**, and **+ g-data** means that the model is further fine-tuned on **g-data**. As shown in Tables 2 and 3, the improvement gap of fine-tuning on **sg-data** from **bsg-data** (3.24% F1) is narrower than that of fine-tuning on **g-data** from **sg-data** (8.84% F1). Fine-tuning on **g-data** may be the key to improve the performance on the test dataset. We believe this is due to the high similarity between

[5]https://nlp.stanford.edu/projects/glove/

	char-LSTM	word-LSTM	char-transformer	word-transformer
all clauses	**85.41**	83.80	81.75	85.10
DRS operators	92.96	93.00	91.67	**93.72**
Roles	**85.03**	82.51	81.22	83.40
Concepts	83.23	81.99	78.89	**83.89**
Synsets-Noun	87.63	87.91	84.34	**89.75**
Verbs	**73.28**	66.38	66.16	68.47
Adjectives	68.92	71.06	62.45	**74.63**
Adverbs	54.55	**83.33**	50.00	40.00

Table 4: F_1-scores of fine-grained evaluation on test dataset.

g-data and the test data. Also, we discover that the model trained on **bsg-data** then fine-tuned on **g-data** can also have good performance, but slightly worse than the final models.

We submitted the word Transformer on **bsg-data + sg-data + g-data** as our final model to the DRS parsing shared task. On the test dataset of the shared task, our model achieves 84.80 F_1 score.

3.3 Analysis

We further analyze the output of the parsers trained on **sg-data + g-data** to see what components of the meaning representation are challenging. Table 4 shows the detailed results of Counter, where DRS Operators (e.g. negation), Roles (e.g. Agent), Concepts (i.e. predicates), synsets (e.g. "n.01") are scored separately.

We compare four parsing models, LSTM with character-level preprocessing (char-LSTM), LSTM with word-level preprocessing (word-LSTM), Transformer with character-level preprocessing (char-transformer) and Transformer with word-level preprocessing (word-transformer). The char-LSTM and word-transformer models both achieve good performance, where word-transformer performs best on the construction of DRS operators, Concepts, Synsets-Noun and Synsets-Adjectives, and char-LSTM performs best on construction of Roles and Synsets-Verbs. The word-LSTM model is mediocre, but significantly outperforms the other models on the construction of Synsets-Adverbs with a large gap of average 35.14% F_1 score.

4 Conclusions

In this paper, we describe the system for the IWCS-2019 Shared Task of DRS parsing. We found that the character-level LSTM and the word-level transformer are competitive in the task. The training time of LSTM models increases as input sequences are longer, while training time are not sensitive to the lengths of input sequences in transformer. The output of LSTM models and transformers have different error distributions. There is still a large improvement space for the sequential models.

Acknowledgments

We thank Hessel Haagsma, Lasha Abzianidze, Rik van Noord and Johan Bos for their release of the latest version of PMB (2.2.0). We gratefully acknowledge the support of the European Research Council (Lapata, Liu; award number 681760), the EU H2020 project SUMMA (Cohen, Liu; grant agreement 688139) and Huawei Technologies (Cohen, Liu).

References

Abzianidze, L., J. Bjerva, K. Evang, H. Haagsma, R. van Noord, P. Ludmann, D.-D. Nguyen, and J. Bos (2017). The parallel meaning bank: Towards a multilingual corpus of translations annotated with compositional meaning representations. In *Proceedings of the 15th Conference of the European Chapter of the Association for Computational Linguistics*, Valencia, Spain, pp. 242–247.

Abzianidze, L., R. van Noord, H. Haagsma, and J. Bos (2019). The first shared task on discourse representation structure parsing. In *Proceedings of the IWCS 2019 Shared Task on Semantic Parsing*.

Bos, J., V. Basile, K. Evang, N. Venhuizen, and J. Bjerva (2017). The groningen meaning bank. In *Handbook of Linguistic Annotation*, pp. 463–496. Springer.

Hochreiter, S. and J. Schmidhuber (1997). Long short-term memory. *Neural Computation*, 1735–1780.

Kamp, H. and U. Reyle (1993). From discourse to logic: An introduction to modeltheoretic semantics of natural language, formal logic and DRT.

Klein, G., Y. Kim, Y. Deng, J. Senellart, and A. M. Rush (2017). OpenNMT: Open-source toolkit for neural machine translation. In *Proceedings of the 55th Annual Meeting of the Association for Computational Linguistics*, Vancouver, Canada, pp. 67–72.

Liu, J., S. B. Cohen, and M. Lapata (2018). Discourse representation structure parsing. In *Proceedings of the 56th Annual Meeting of the Association for Computational Linguistics*, Melbourne, Australia, pp. 429–439.

Pennington, J., R. Socher, and C. D. Manning (2014). Glove: Global vectors for word representation. In *Empirical Methods in Natural Language Processing (EMNLP)*, pp. 1532–1543.

van Noord, R., L. Abzianidze, H. Haagsma, and J. Bos (2018). Evaluating scoped meaning representations. In *Proceedings of the Eleventh International Conference on Language Resources and Evaluation*, Miyazaki, Japan, pp. 1685–1693.

van Noord, R., L. Abzianidze, A. Toral, and J. Bos (2018). Exploring neural methods for parsing discourse representation structures. *Transactions of the Association for Computational Linguistics*, 619–633.

Vaswani, A., N. Shazeer, N. Parmar, J. Uszkoreit, L. Jones, A. N. Gomez, Ł. Kaiser, and I. Polosukhin (2017). Attention is all you need. In *Advances in Neural Information Processing Systems*, pp. 5998–6008.

Neural Boxer at the IWCS Shared Task on DRS Parsing

Rik van Noord
Center for Language and Cognition, University of Groningen
r.i.k.van.noord@rug.nl

Abstract

This paper describes our participation in the shared task of Discourse Representation Structure parsing. It follows the work of Van Noord et al. (2019), who employed a neural sequence-to-sequence model to produce DRSs, also exploiting linguistic information with multiple encoders. We provide a detailed look in the performance of this model and show that (i) the benefit of the linguistic features is evident across a number of experiments which vary the amount of training data and (ii) the model can be improved by applying a number of postprocessing methods to fix ill-formed output. Our model ended up in second place in the competition, with an F-score of 84.5.

1 Introduction

Semantic parsing is the problem of mapping natural language utterances to interpretable meaning representations. Specifically, we focus on producing Discourse Representation Structures (DRS), based on Discourse Representation Theory (Kamp, 1984; Kamp and Reyle, 1993), a formalism developed in formal semantics. Since DRS parsing is a complex task, among others dealing with scope, negation, presuppositions and discourse structures, previous parsers used to be a combination of symbolic and statistical components (Bos, 2008, 2015). However, recently neural sequence-to-sequence models achieved impressive performance on the task (Liu et al., 2018; Van Noord et al., 2018, 2019).

This work describes our system with which we participated in the first shared task on DRS parsing (Abzianidze et al., 2019). Our system is the same as described in Van Noord et al. (2019), except for a number of additional post-processing methods to solve ill-formed DRSs. Van Noord et al. (2019) follow Van Noord et al. (2018) in employing a sequence-to-sequence neural network to produce the DRSs, using character-level input[1] and rewriting the variables to a more general structure. They then improve on this work by exploiting linguistic information (POS-tags, semantic tags[2], dependency parses, CCG categories and lemmas), using a second encoder to provide this information to the model. We first demonstrate how sensitive the model is to changes in certain parameter settings, after which we determine if the model could still benefit from additional gold or silver standard data (Section 2). In Section 3, we describe our new postprocessing methods to decrease the number of ill-formed DRSs. Finally in Section 4 we perform a detailed error analysis.

2 Analysis

All results are obtained by training on the data released in Parallel Meaning Bank release 2.2.0 (Abzianidze et al., 2017). This release contains gold standard (fully manually annotated) data of which we use 4,597 as train, 682 as dev and 650 as test instances. Moreover, we also use the 67,965 silver (partly manually annotated) instances as extra training data for some experiments. Reported values are F-scores calculated by COUNTER (Van Noord, Abzianidze, Haagsma, and Bos, 2018), which are averaged over 3

[1] They use *super characters* (Van Noord and Bos, 2017a,b) for DRS roles and operators.

[2] See Bjerva et al. (2016) and Abzianidze and Bos (2017) for a detailed description of semantic tagging.

different runs of the system. In this section, all experiments are performed on the development set. All code is publicly available.[3]

2.1 Parameter sensitivity

The parameter search in Van Noord et al. (2019) was performed by applying a hill climbing method: one parameter was tuned with all other parameters fixed. Only if a parameter returned a significant improvement, it was chosen over the current setting. In Van Noord et al. (2019) we only did a single pass over all parameters, meaning that there is likely still room for improvement. Also, it is interesting to determine the sensitivity of our model to certain parameter settings, since we generally prefer a model that is not too sensitive to slight changes in them.

We performed a detailed search for the hyper-parameters RNN dimension, dropout, learning rate and beam size, of which the results are shown in Figure 1.[4] We see that the model allows for some variety in dropout and learning rate, though there is a sharp decrease in performance if we move too far from the optimal setting. For the RNN dimension there is not much difference if more than 250 nodes are used, though increasing the dimension to 500 could improve performance. Similarly, a beam size of 5 is sufficient for good performance, but using a beam size of 15 could be an extra small gain.

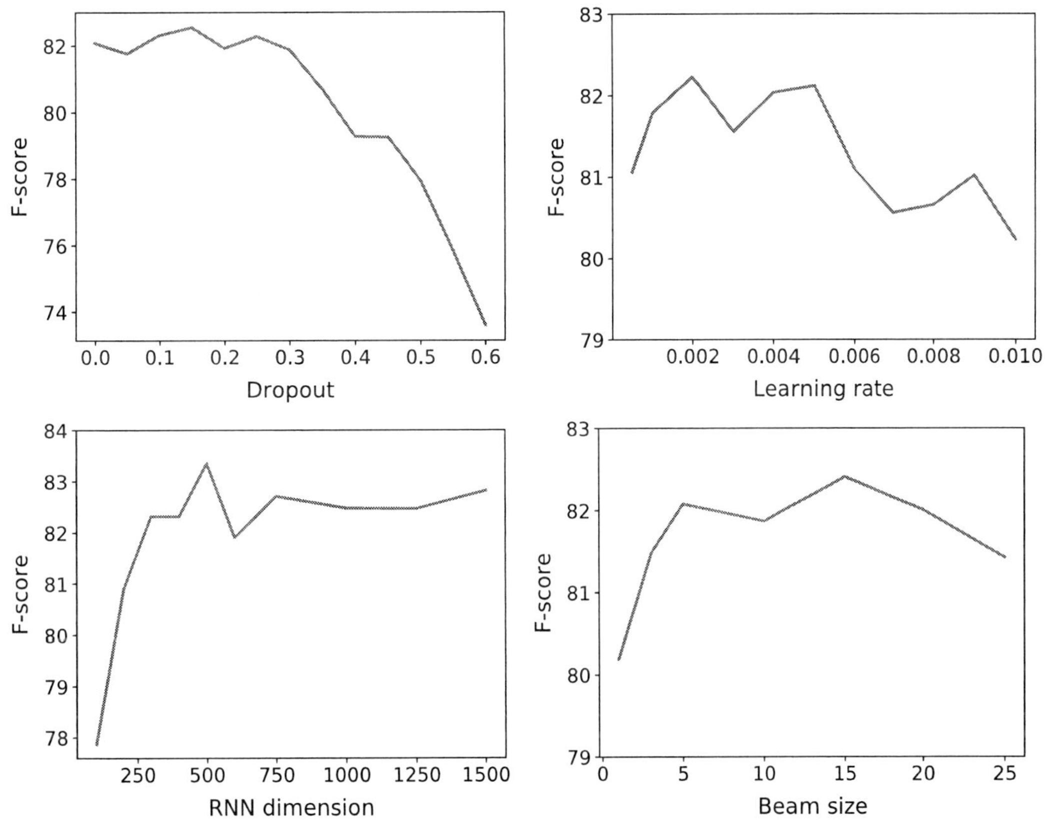

Figure 1: Performance of our best model trained on only gold standard data for the hyper parameters (shared task setting in brackets): RNN dimensions (300), dropout (0.2), learning rate (0.002) and beam size (10).

[3]https://github.com/RikVN/Neural_DRS

[4]Performed after the shared task deadline, our official scores are with the parameters reported in Van Noord et al. (2019).

2.2 Learning curves

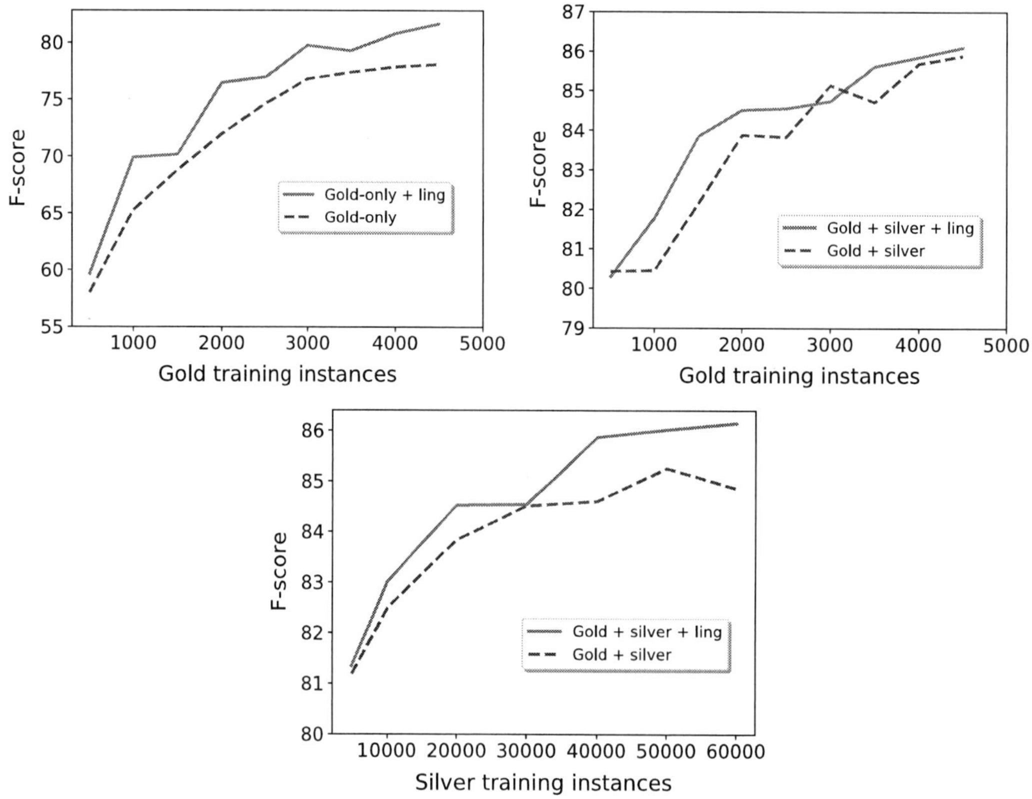

Figure 2: Performance of our baseline and best system for: training on only different amounts of gold data (top left), training on all silver standard data with different amounts of gold data (top right), and training on different amounts of silver data, finetuned on all gold data (bottom).

Since manual DRS annotation is a hard and time consuming task, it is interesting to know how much we can still benefit from extra silver and gold standard examples, as well as identifying how the amount of data contributes to the final scores. Concurrently, we can also observe the impact of the linguistic features across different amounts of training data. We show the learning curves of two models: the baseline model and the best model. The best model employs the linguistic features in a separate encoder.

How much gold is needed?
The top-left graph of Figure 2 (left) shows the performance of our two models when only using gold training data. It is clear that additional gold data still improves performance, though in a way we already knew this due to the success of employing silver data. Therefore, we also plot the effect of varying the amount of gold data used when using all available silver data in the top right graph of Figure 2. We see the same trend there: adding gold standard data still clearly improves performance.

How much silver is needed?
The effect of varying the amount of silver data is shown in bottom graph of Figure 2. The initial addition of silver data is clearly beneficial. However, the effect seems to diminish a bit for the best model after 40,000 silver instances. The baseline model, though, still improves after 40,000 instances. In general, it seems like additional silver data could be beneficial, though the extra benefit is likely to be small.

Impact of linguistic features
For all experiments shown in Figure 2, we see that the linguistic features increase performance across virtually all amounts of data used. This further confirms that the linguistic features supply the model with additional useful information.

3 Postprocessing methods

There are a number of syntactic and semantic requirements for a set of clauses to be considered a well-formed DRS (Van Noord et al., 2018). Among others, there should be a single main box and there should be no loop in the subordination of boxes. Since we do not restrict our model when producing clauses, these errors can occur. However, they can often be (easily) fixed, by changing a single clause or a set of clauses. We outline a few of those methods below. Moreover, we propose a method to improve performance on word sense disambiguation.

3.1 Improvement methods

Removing clauses
One of the problems of the neural model is that it can get stuck in a loop producing (more or less) the same output. We apply two straightforward methods to fix these instances. For one, we remove all clauses after clause number 75. Second, we remove clauses of concepts, roles and operators (except `REF`) if they occur more than three times. We only look at the second argument of a clause (the identifier), for example, if a full DRS contains five `Theme` clauses, we remove the last two, no matter the other values in those clauses.

No main box found
If there is no main box found, this means that there are multiple independent boxes. For two independent boxes, we first try to remedy this by changing a single discourse variable in one of these boxes. We change a discourse variable that is unique in **b1** to a unique variable in **b2** (and vice versa), to establish a connection between the boxes. For each of these possible changes we check whether the DRS is well-formed now, and if so, return the new DRS. For multiple independent boxes, and if the previous method failed for two independent boxes, we start merging boxes together (e.g. replace each occurrence of **b1** by **b2**), until we find a well-formed DRS. If this does not result in a well-formed DRS, we return a non-matching dummy DRS.[5]

Subordinate relation has a loop
This can occur if boxes indirectly subordinate themselves, e.g. **b0** subordinates **b1**, **b1** subordinates **b2** and **b2** subordinates **b0**. To solve this, we first try to merge the offending box with each of the other boxes in the DRS. If this does not work, we try to remove the offending box from the DRS. If the DRS is still ill-formed, we start the process again if the error is *Subordinate relation has a loop* (but now with the offending box removed) or apply the previously described fix for *No main box found*. A non-matching dummy DRS is returned if the DRS is still ill-formed after these steps.[5]

Fixing senses
Previous work showed that the neural model often produced the wrong word sense for the correct concept (Van Noord et al., 2018). It even often output senses that were never observed in the training set. We apply a simple method to fix these instances. If a concept + sense is not present in the gold standard training set, we replace the sense by the most frequent sense for this concept in the training set. For example, we change `grow.v.01` to `grow.v.07` and `fast.n.02` to `fast.a.02`. Note that this method does not influence whether a DRS is well-formed or not. This was implemented after the shared task deadline, meaning our final shared task system did not apply this method.

[5]The shared task system returned the SPAR default DRS.

3.2 Results

We can check by how much the scores in Van Noord et al. (2019) would have improved if these methods had been applied. The results of adding the improvement methods incrementally are shown in Table 1. We see that simply removing clauses returns only modest gains, but fixing ill-formed DRSs gives a substantial improvement, even for our best model. By applying these fixes on the shared task evaluation set we decreased the number of ill-formed DRSs from 283 to 9, but since this evaluation set was not released, we do not know the impact on the F-score. The method for fixing word senses also proved quite effective, improving the final F-score by 0.2 to 0.4.

	Initial		+ Removing clauses		+ Solving ill-formed		+ Fixing senses	
	ill (%)	F1	ill (%)	F1	ill (%)	F1	ill (%)	F1
Gold-only baseline	2.6	78.6	2.6	78.8	0.2	79.5	0.2	79.8
Gold-only + ling	2.7	81.3	2.7	81.4	0.1	82.2	0.1	82.4
Gold + silver + ling	1.5	84.5	1.5	84.5	0.0	85.1	0.0	85.4
Gold + silver + ling	0.9	85.6	0.9	85.7	0.0	86.1	0.0	86.4

Table 1: Impact of the new postprocessing methods on the dev set results of Van Noord et al. (2019).

4 Results & Error Analysis

4.1 Detailed F-scores

The right column of Table 2 shows the results of our official submission to the shared task. We obtained an F-score of 84.5, with a precision and recall of 85.5 and 83.6, which is slightly lower than our dev and test scores. We ended up in second place in the competition, though the difference with the first place (84.8) was not statistically significant.

Table 2 also contains the automatically calculated detailed F-scores on the test set for both Van Noord et al. (2018) and Van Noord et al. (2019). The improvement for the new neural model and the addition of the linguistic features mainly comes from improved performance on the roles and concepts. It is evident that word sense disambiguation is a hard problem, since even with our method to fix word senses, we still obtain large increases in F-score for oracle senses. The improvement methods described in Section 3 result in a modest, but significant 0.4 increase on the test set.

	NeuDRS-18	NeuDRS-19	This work - test	This work - eval
All clauses	83.2	87.0	87.4	84.5
DRS Operators	93.4	94.4	94.5	94.2
VerbNet roles	83.2	87.1	87.3	83.5
WordNet synsets	79.7	84.3	85.2	82.3
nouns	85.5	89.3	90.1	87.5
verbs	65.6	72.2	73.0	68.9
adjectives	64.7	70.4	73.6	74.2
adverbs	50.0	72.6	71.9	45.5
Oracle sense numbers	85.7	89.2	89.6	87.1
Oracle synsets	90.0	92.6	92.7	90.7
Oracle roles	86.7	90.0	90.4	88.5

Table 2: F-scores of fine-grained evaluation on the test set of the work of Van Noord et al. (2018) (NeuDRS-18) , Van Noord et al. (2019) (NeuDRS-19) and this work, which is NeuDRS-19 plus the improvement methods described in Section 3.

4.2 Examples

Relatively good performance	Relatively bad performance
(a) Tom died when he was 97.	(f) These bananas are not ripe.
(b) I read comic books.	(g) A book about dancing is lying on the desk.
(c) We should drink 64 ounces of fluids a day.	(h) Approximately seven billion people inhabit our planet.
(d) I look down on liars and cheats.	(i) The trip will take approximately five hours.
(e) You can't run away.	(j) Tom was too tired to speak.

Table 3: Sentences for which our model performed relatively well and poor.

The organizers provided us with five sentences in the test set for which our model did relatively well, and 5 for which the model performed relatively poor. The sentences are shown in Table 3.[6] Interestingly, the model does well on sentences containing numbers, (a) and (c), but fails to capture the correct interpretation of *approximately* in (h) and (j). For (b) and (d), our model correctly identified the multi-word expressions *comic_book* and *look_down_on*, perhaps due to the character-level input. For (e), our model produced a perfect DRS, while other approaches had trouble either producing *run_away*, or the fact that the sentence was addressed to a hearer. Sentence (j) is interpreted in the gold standard as *Tom could not speak because he was tired*, which our model simply failed to capture. It produced a DRS more similar to the meaning of *Tom spoke and was tired*, as is shown in Table 4.

Gold standard		Produced output	Matching
b2 REF **x1**	**b6** DRS **b1**	**b1** REF **x1**	**b2** ⇒ **b1**
b2 Name **x1** "tom"	**b6** DRS **b3**	**b1** Name **x1** "tom"	**x1** ⇒ **x1**
b2 male "n.02" **x1**	**b6** RESULT **b1** **b3**	**b1** male "n.02" **x1**	**b1** ⇒ **b2**
b1 REF **t1**	**b1** REF **s1**	**b2** REF **x2**	**t1** ⇒ **x2**
b1 TPR **t1** "now"	**b1** Theme **s1** **x1**	**b2** TPR **x2** "now"	**s1** ⇒ **x3**
b1 Time **s1** **t1**	**b1** tired "a.01" **s1**	**b2** Time **x3** **x2**	**b3** ⇒ ∅
b1 time "n.08" **t1**	**b5** REF **e1**	**b2** time "n.08" **x2**	**b4** ⇒ ∅
b3 NOT **b4**	**b5** Agent **e1** **x1**	**b2** REF **x3**	**b5** ⇒ ∅
b4 POS **b5**	**b5** speak "v.01" **e1**	**b2** Theme **x3** **x1**	**b6** ⇒ ∅
		b2 tired "a.01" **x3**	**e1** ⇒ ∅
		b2 Co-Theme **x3** **x4**	∅ ⇒ **x4**
		b2 REF **x4**	
		b2 speak "n.01" **x4**	

Table 4: Gold standard and produced DRS for the sentence *Tom was too tired to speak.* This gave us a precision and recall of $7/9$ and $7/14$, resulting in an F-score of 0.61.

5 Conclusion

This paper provided a more detailed analysis on the study of Van Noord et al. (2019), in which they showed that explicitly encoder linguistic features can be beneficial for neural sequence-to-sequence models on the task of DRS parsing. We show that the benefit of these features are robust across experiments with different amounts of training data. Moreover, we show that the model is not too sensitive to small variations in parameter settings, perhaps even observing room for more finetuning of the model. Lastly, we show that a number of rule-based methods can drastically decrease the number of ill-formed DRSs. Our method ultimately obtained a second place in the shared task competition with an F-score of 84.5.

[6]DRSs available at: https://urd2.let.rug.nl/ rikvannoord/DRS/IWCS/

Acknowledgements

This work was funded by the NWO-VICI grant "Lost in Translation – Found in Meaning" (288-89-003). The Tesla K40 GPU used in this work was kindly donated to us by the NVIDIA Corporation.

References

Abzianidze, L., J. Bjerva, K. Evang, H. Haagsma, R. van Noord, P. Ludmann, D.-D. Nguyen, and J. Bos (2017, April). The Parallel Meaning Bank: Towards a multilingual corpus of translations annotated with compositional meaning representations. In *Proceedings of the 15th Conference of the European Chapter of the Association for Computational Linguistics: Volume 2, Short Papers*, Valencia, Spain, pp. 242–247. Association for Computational Linguistics.

Abzianidze, L. and J. Bos (2017, September). Towards universal semantic tagging. In *Proceedings of the 12th International Conference on Computational Semantics (IWCS 2017) – Short Papers*, Montpellier, France, pp. 307–313. Association for Computational Linguistics.

Abzianidze, L., R. van Noord, H. Haagsma, and J. Bos (2019). The first shared task on discourse representation structure parsing. In *Proceedings of the IWCS 2019 Shared Task on Semantic Parsing*.

Bjerva, J., B. Plank, and J. Bos (2016). Semantic tagging with deep residual networks. In *Proceedings of COLING 2016, the 26th International Conference on Computational Linguistics: Technical Papers*, Osaka, Japan, pp. 3531–3541.

Bos, J. (2008). Wide-coverage semantic analysis with Boxer. In *Semantics in Text Processing. STEP 2008 Conference Proceedings*, Volume 1 of *Research in Computational Semantics*, pp. 277–286. Venice, Italy: College Publications.

Bos, J. (2015). Open-domain semantic parsing with Boxer. In B. Megyesi (Ed.), *Proceedings of the 20th Nordic Conference of Computational Linguistics (NODALIDA 2015)*, Vilnius, Lithuania, pp. 301–304.

Kamp, H. (1984). A theory of truth and semantic representation. In J. Groenendijk, T. M. Janssen, and M. Stokhof (Eds.), *Truth, Interpretation and Information*, pp. 1–41. Dordrecht – Holland/Cinnaminson – U.S.A.: FORIS.

Kamp, H. and U. Reyle (1993). *From Discourse to Logic; An Introduction to Modeltheoretic Semantics of Natural Language, Formal Logic and DRT*. Dordrecht: Kluwer.

Liu, J., S. B. Cohen, and M. Lapata (2018). Discourse representation structure parsing. In *Proceedings of the 56th Annual Meeting of the Association for Computational Linguistics (Volume 1: Long Papers)*, Volume 1, Melbourne, Australia, pp. 429–439.

Van Noord, R., L. Abzianidze, H. Haagsma, and J. Bos (2018). Evaluating scoped meaning representations. In *Proceedings of the Eleventh International Conference on Language Resources and Evaluation (LREC 2018)*, Paris, France, pp. 1685–1693. European Language Resources Association (ELRA).

Van Noord, R., L. Abzianidze, A. Toral, and J. Bos (2018). Exploring neural methods for parsing discourse representation structures. *Transactions of the Association for Computational Linguistics 6*, 619–633.

Van Noord, R. and J. Bos (2017a). Dealing with co-reference in neural semantic parsing. In *Proceedings of the 2nd Workshop on Semantic Deep Learning (SemDeep-2)*, Montpellier, France, pp. 41–49.

Van Noord, R. and J. Bos (2017b). Neural semantic parsing by character-based translation: Experiments with abstract meaning representations. *Computational Linguistics in the Netherlands Journal 7*, 93–108.

Van Noord, R., A. Toral, and J. Bos (2019). Linguistic information in neural semantic parsing with multiple encoders. In *IWCS 2019-13th International Conference on Computational Semantics-Short papers*.

Association for Computational Linguistics
209 N. Eighth Street
Stroudsburg, Pennsylvania 18360

ISBN 978-1-5108-8766-4

9 781510 887664

CURRAN ASSOCIATES INC.
proceedings.com